LANDSCAPES OF EXPLORATION

EDITED BY LIZ WELLS

UPP
University of Plymouth Press

This edition first published in the United Kingdom in 2012 by
University of Plymouth Press, Roland Levinsky Building, Drake Circus,
Plymouth, Devon, PL4 8AA, United Kingdom.

ISBN 978-1-84102-301-4

A CIP catalogue record of this book is available from the British Library

Publisher: Paul Honeywill
Design: Daniel Jones & Steven Bond

Printed and bound by Short Run Press, Exeter, Devon

Cover image courtesy NASA/MODIS Rapid Response System, Antarctica Project.

FSC www.fsc.org
MIX
Paper from responsible sources
FSC® C014540

The history of Plymouth University is suffused with ideas of exploration and discovery, growing out of a rich educational heritage that dates from the founding of the Plymouth School of Navigation in 1862. The university's coat of arms incorporates the dictum *Indagate, Fingite, Invenite* – Explore, Dream, Discover, reflecting not only Plymouth's long and continuing association with seafarers and explorers, but also its current ambitions for its students and staff. As the university celebrates 150 years of higher education in the city, it continues to champion the enterprise of enquiry which fosters innovation, including new research collaborations, for example, between the arts and the University's Marine Institute, a leading international research centre in marine sciences.

The public arts programme of the university, Peninsula Arts, offers a year-round platform for cultural events, including exhibitions, music, film, public lectures, theatre and dance. Situated within a broad-based, multi-discipline university, Peninsula Arts has a particular interest in supporting creative initiatives which explore the relationship between art, science and technology. Peninsula Arts' programming draws direct inspiration from the expertise and specialist knowledge of researchers and practitioners working across a range of art and science subjects. This collaborative approach to stimulating new knowledge ensures that the cultural programme has a currency and a critical edge. It brings to the South West an international network of artists and experts, recognised for their significant contributions to their field – as well as encouraging emerging voices whose fresh perspectives provoke new insight.

As the University celebrates its 150th anniversary, Peninsula Arts is delighted to showcase the exhibition Landscapes of Exploration. Curated by Liz Wells, Professor in Photographic Culture in the School of Art & Media, the exhibition features the work of artists whose practice in visual art, music and writing, reflects on the physical and conceptual impact of working in the remote and very special environment of Antarctica. The title *Landscapes of Exploration* perhaps belies the determined, tenacious spirit of enquiry essential to working in such extreme locations, but does evoke a sense of discovery, of imagining – then confronting – the unknown, which has been typical of this kind of human endeavour over the centuries.

It is fitting, therefore, that the exhibition should begin in Plymouth in 2012, as the city and university mark the centenary of Captain Robert Falcon Scott's historic expedition to the South Pole. Born and educated in Plymouth, Scott's story, despite its tragic conclusion, epitomises the physical courage, the mental endurance – but above all the belief in the possible – so necessary to embark on such a venture. *Indagate, Fingite, Invenite...*

Professor David Coslett
Executive Dean, Faculty of Arts
Plymouth University

\+ Alongside the exhibition, Peninsula Arts is hosting *True South*, a two-day festival, which brings together artists and scientists, whose work explores the scientific, environmental and philosophical significance of Antarctica.

CONTENTS

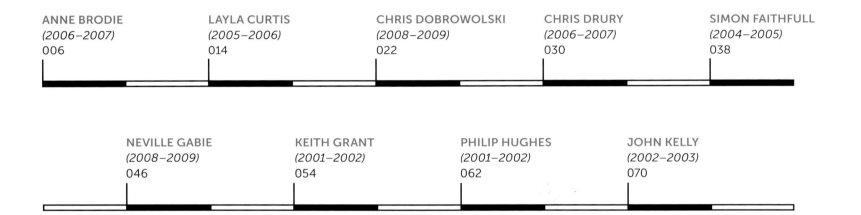

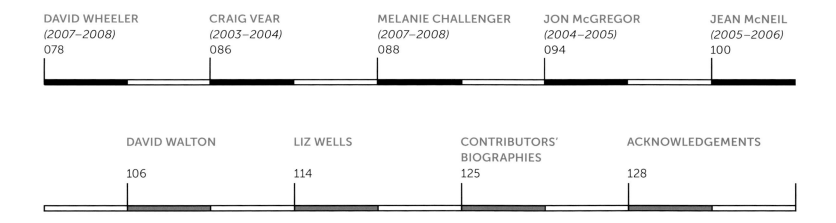

Most people watching *Breathing Berg* for the first time make an assumption that it has been digitally manipulated. We have grown so accustomed to the slick tricks of the advertising industry that we find it hard to believe that something so unworldly can in fact be real. My part in making the film was to be a witness with a film camera and to make the decision to edit the sound using footage from the previous day's filming. The iceberg struggles to find its balance. Every aspect of the Antarctic environment, and every aspect of being alive in such extreme conditions, feels difficult and precarious.

+ **Breathing Berg,** *2007, DVD, 2 mins 57 secs*

ANNE BRODIE *(2006–2007)*

Gin and Tonic was filmed in the bar on board a British Antarctic Survey (BAS) ship, the *James Clark Ross,* as we crossed the Convergence Zone into the Antarctic Circle. The outside temperature dropped six degrees in just over an hour and the first icebergs could be seen in the distance.

The scale of where I was and the enormity of the task of being an artist in such an overwhelming environment began to intimidate me. I needed to work out a way in which to filter the experience into more manageable human proportions and I retreated inside to the ship's bar. The passage to Antarctica can be equally read in the movement of my gin and tonic with its miniature ice cube, as in the giant seas outside going through Drake Passage.

+ Gin and Tonic (crossing the Convergence Zone and Drake Passage), *2007, DVD, 2 mins 57 secs*

While the scientists interacted with the environment using scientific instruments of measurement to bring back physical and electronic samples and data, it became the individual's unique human connection with the Antarctic environment that came to inform my work. I felt an important point was being overlooked; Antarctica is about us. I felt we should be utilising and embracing our heightened 'humanness' that the extraordinary polar environment invokes, alongside the more rigid scientific data collecting that objectively filters this out.

I asked the inhabitants of the British Antarctic Base at Rothera, among whom I had been living and working for nearly three months, to anonymously fill small glass collection jars with whatever they felt best represented their identity and feelings in Antarctica. The temporary inhabitants of the Antarctic Peninsula returned them filled with a hugely imaginative range of substances, ranging from skidoo chain links to blood and pornography. A different kind of data collection.

+
Suturing thread and needle
From: outgoing base doctor.
Dentist's drill used to etch message on the bottle.

"And here is a jar full of many different lengths of line"

+
Blood
From: a pilot.

"Antarctica. A choice"

+
Birthday candles, 'no cheese' message
From: base chef.

"Cyril need or not need
Chef like or not like"

Antarctic ice block

Commissioned by Arts Catalyst, the melting ice block was shown at the Society of Antiquaries, Burlington House, Piccadilly, London, to coincide with the launch of the book *Bipolar,* as the culmination of the Polar Programme, an interdisciplinary polar archive created for International Polar Year 2007–2008.

Artist Anne Brodie took one of the lumps of ice that she had brought back from Antarctica out of its lodgings inside the British Antarctic Survey's freezer in Cambridge, UK, and let it not-so-gently melt over the course of the evening. The ice was acoustically wired, and produced uncomfortably loud interruptions of noise as the ancient gas, kept locked under pressure, escaped and belched into the London air. The cabinet was recycled from an exhibition in the British Museum.

Dug up by the artist and a BAS scientist, from a deep-field glacier, the ice piggybacked to the UK among the scientific ice. Unlike the scientific ice cores, which from the outset have a predetermined course and data gathering objective, bringing this ice back poses many questions about the role of sentiment, subjectivity and emotional attachment to the Antarctic environment, particularly if our only experience of it is through the interface of film and photography.

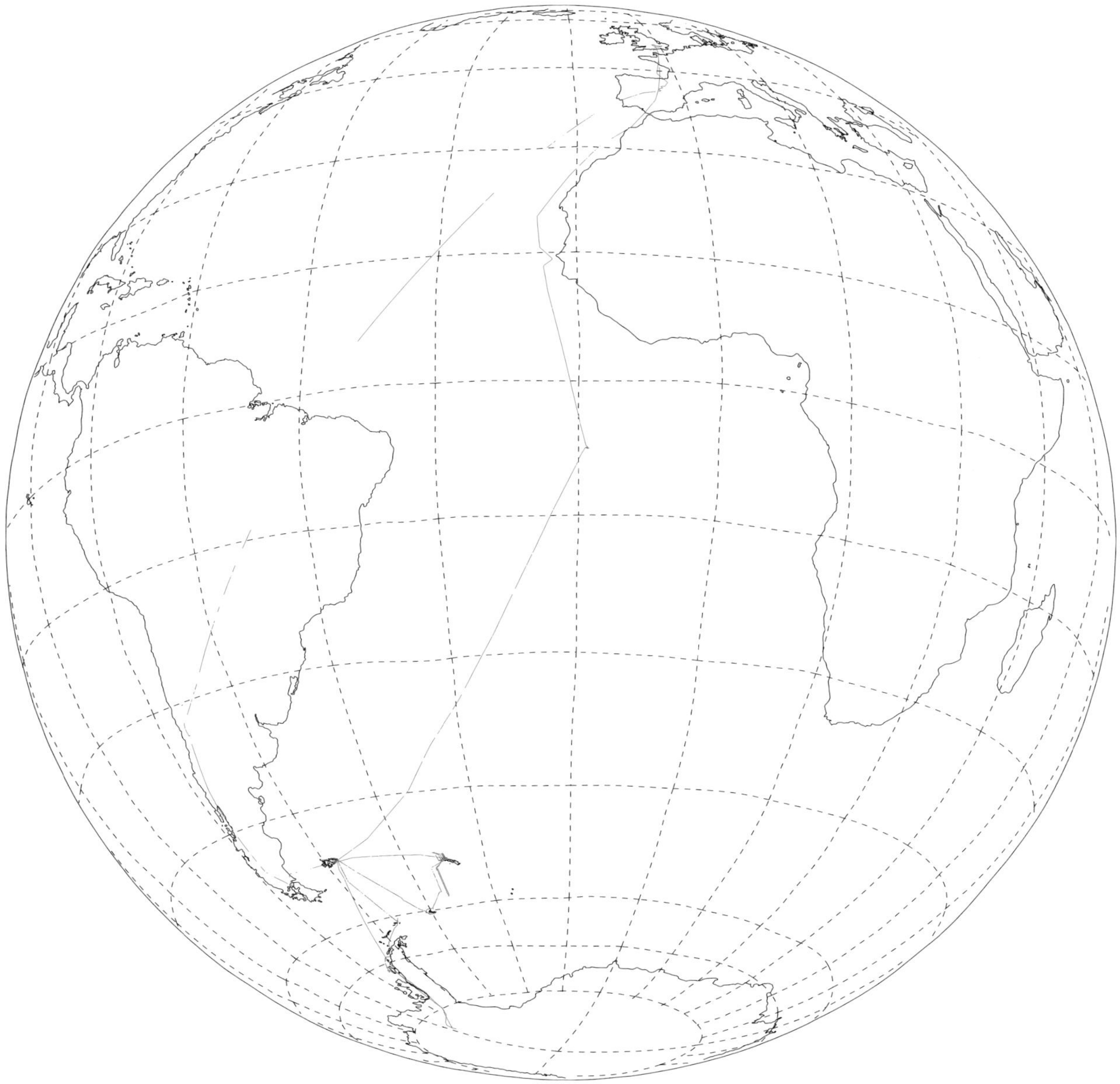

+ **Polar Wandering,** *2005–2006,* Internet-based interactive drawing with photographs, http://www.polarwandering.co.uk

THATCHER DRIVE

LAYLA CURTIS *(2005–2006)*

+ King Edward Point, South Georgia; 54.283°S 36.496°W, 81 hours 3 minutes 4 seconds; 30.2 miles, *2006,* Silkscreen print, 95 x 95 cm

\+ Choiseul Sound, Falkland Islands; 51.956°S 58.580°W; 8 hours 34 minutes 20 seconds; 15.3 miles, *2006,* Silkscreen print, 95 x 95 cm

+ **78 Degrees North, 67 Degrees South,** *2007,* Two channel video (animated webcam stills), colour, silent

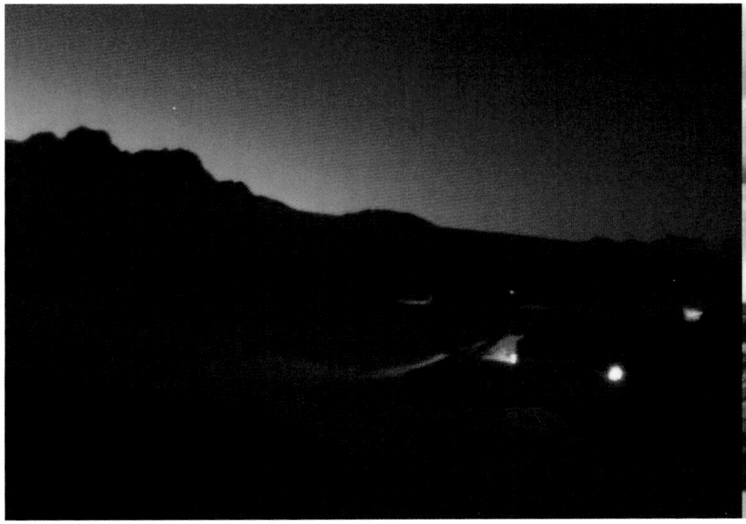

+ **Wanderers,** *2006,* Video projection, colour, silent, 28 mins 18 secs

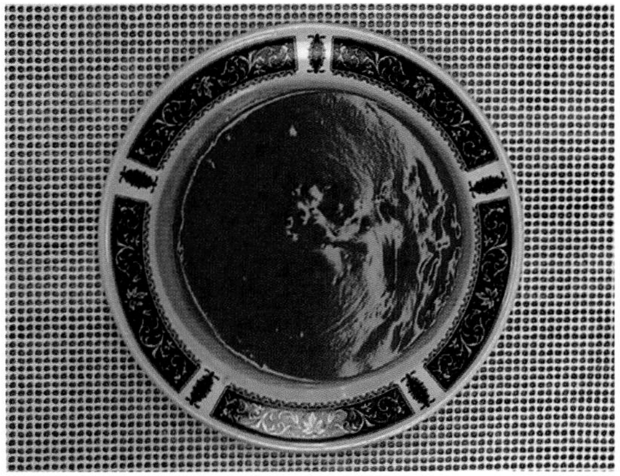

Layla Curtis spent three months in the Antarctic. Her seven-week journey on the *RRS James Clark Ross* took her from Stanley in the Falkland Islands to three of the British Antarctic Survey's research stations: Signy Island, Bird Island and King Edward Point on South Georgia. Later, on arriving on the Antarctic Peninsula, she used Rothera Research Station as a base to travel further into the field. She subsequently visited Fossil Bluff, spent a week camping (and unloading and refuelling aircraft) at Sky Blu, and co-piloted a Twin Otter aeroplane to the Ellsworth Mountains.

During her time on board the ice-strengthened ship, Curtis created some of her first works in video. *Soup*, a portrait of a bowl of Heinz tomato soup as seen directly from above, was filmed during a storm as the ship journeyed through Drake Passage. The two channel video projection *Horizons (Port, Starboard)*, also inspired by the violent rolling of the vessel, depicts the moving horizon line filmed simultaneously from opposite sides of the ship. The slower-paced *Ice Floes* was filmed once the *JCR* began to crunch through thick pack ice further south.

Curtis continually recorded her entire 90-day journey using a hand-held Global Positioning System (GPS). As her journey unfolded, she uploaded longitudinal and latitudinal data from the tracking device to her custom-built project website – www.polarwandering.co.uk – along with photographs she took en route. *Polar Wandering* continuously charted her progress and the positional data, represented on the website by a thin red line, eventually grew into a 27,856 mile-long interactive web-based drawing, populated with over 1,000 photographs. A suite of 10 limited edition screen prints, focussing on specific points and incidents within the drawing, was also produced.

Other works created during her residency include *Wanderers*, a video depicting a bird-filled misty sky as seen through the window of an isolated scientist's hut at an albatross colony on Bird Island; and *Crevasse*, a two channel video installation depicting a gradual assent out of an Antarctic crevasse. The time-lapse work *78 Degrees North, 67 Degrees South*, which compiles images transmitted over the course of one year, from two webcams situated at scientific research stations located at opposite ends of the planet, was created a year after the artist's return to the UK.

Layla Curtis' Antarctic works were developed in collaboration with Locus+.

+ **Soup**, *2006*, Video, colour, silent, 18 mins 25 secs

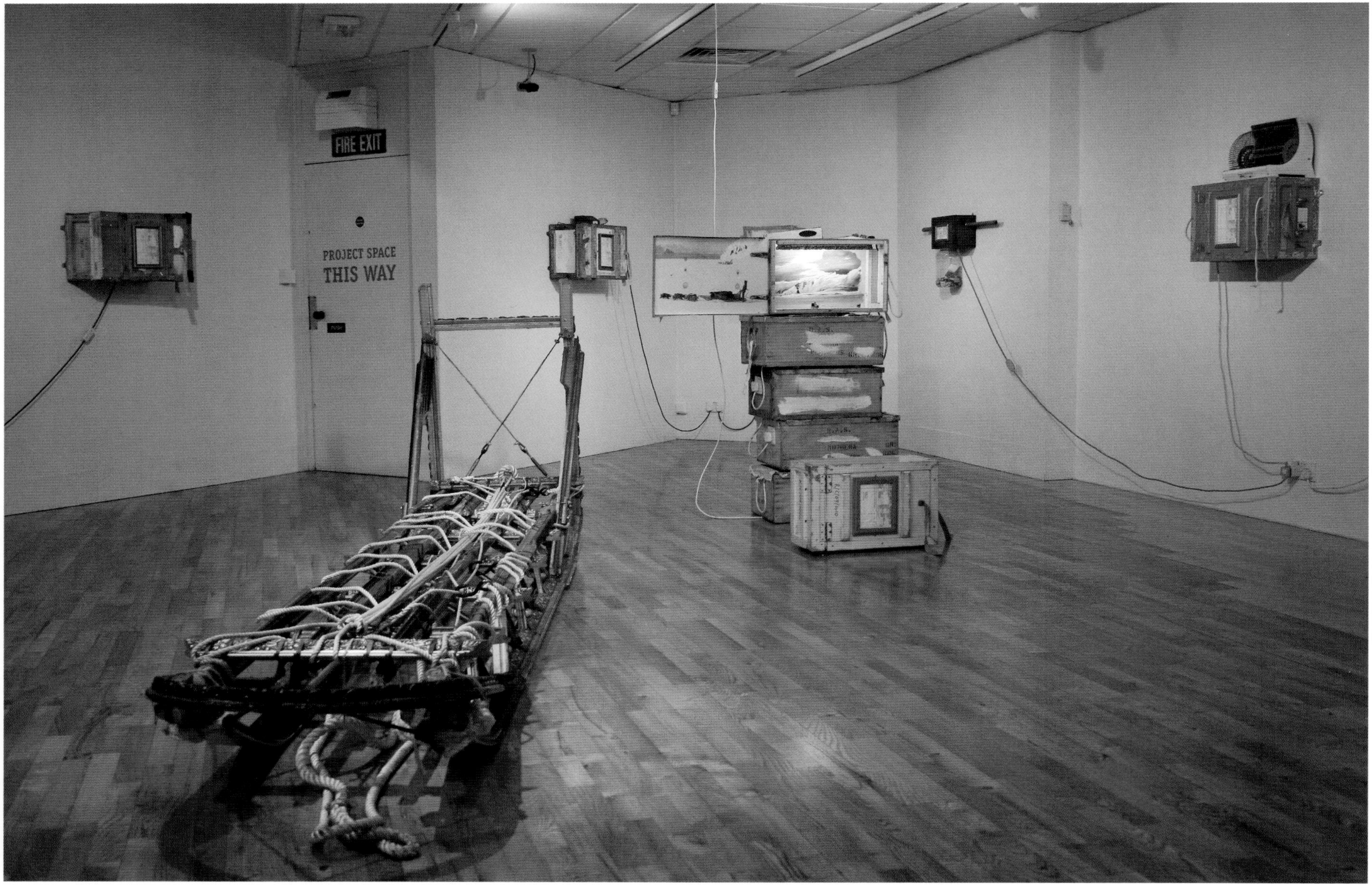

+ **Gold picture frame sledge,** *2010,* Installed at the Essex University Gallery, photograph M. Bowman

Dobrowolski took art references with him – in the form of gilt picture frames that he packed into boxes and transported for construction on arrival into a traditional 'Nansen' design sledge.

The installation consists of Dobrowolski's sledge and boxes, developed as art pieces, in which his observations of scenes from life in the Antarctic play out. Each box contains an assembly of objects referencing expeditions past and present, in ways that are at once humourous, engaging and thought provoking.

∧+ Linked travel, Sledge teams operating away from base, roped together in tandem
+ Food depot, A stack of 'man food' boxes at Sky Blu
>+ Gold picture frame sledge, First time on snow, photograph Reuters

+ **Gold picture frame sledge and construction details,** Near McCallum Pass, Wright Peninsula, Adelaide Island, photographs F. Buckley & Gaby

+ **Discarded sledge box**, Used by the BAS headquarters in Britain to ship some of the gold picture frames down to Rothera, Antarctica

1

2

3

4

5

1 **Child's book,** *Captain Scott,* a Ladybird book from the 1960s
2 **Sledge box,** Full of children's Antarctic toys in the Antarctic
3 **Untitled,** Oil paint, sledge box, camera tripod, toy skidoo and cameraman figure, Essex University Gallery
4 **Untitled,** Oil paint, sledge box, toy van and snow track, tape recording describing the taste of penguin, Essex University Gallery
5 **Toy sledge in the Antarctic**

2

1

3

4

1 **Untitled,** Oil paint, sledge box, 1950s vacuum cleaner, model aeroplane, broken camera, image of model and vacuum cleaner in the Antarctic, Essex University Gallery
2 **Untitled,** Sledge box, eight assorted slide viewers, collection of toy Antarctic figures, images of them on slide in the Antarctic, Essex University Gallery
3 **Untitled,** Detail of painting in sledge box, toy figures and miniature television, film footage of the gold picture frame sledge, Essex University Gallery
4 **Untitled,** Oil paint, sledge box, plastic toy penguin, image of toy penguin in South Georgia, Essex University Gallery

\+ **Gold picture frame sledge,** Making camp just outside Sky Blu, photo F. Buckley
\>+ **Gold picture frame sledge,** Returning to base after an early trial near Rothera., photo F. Buckley

INSIDE TENT
UNIT No 8

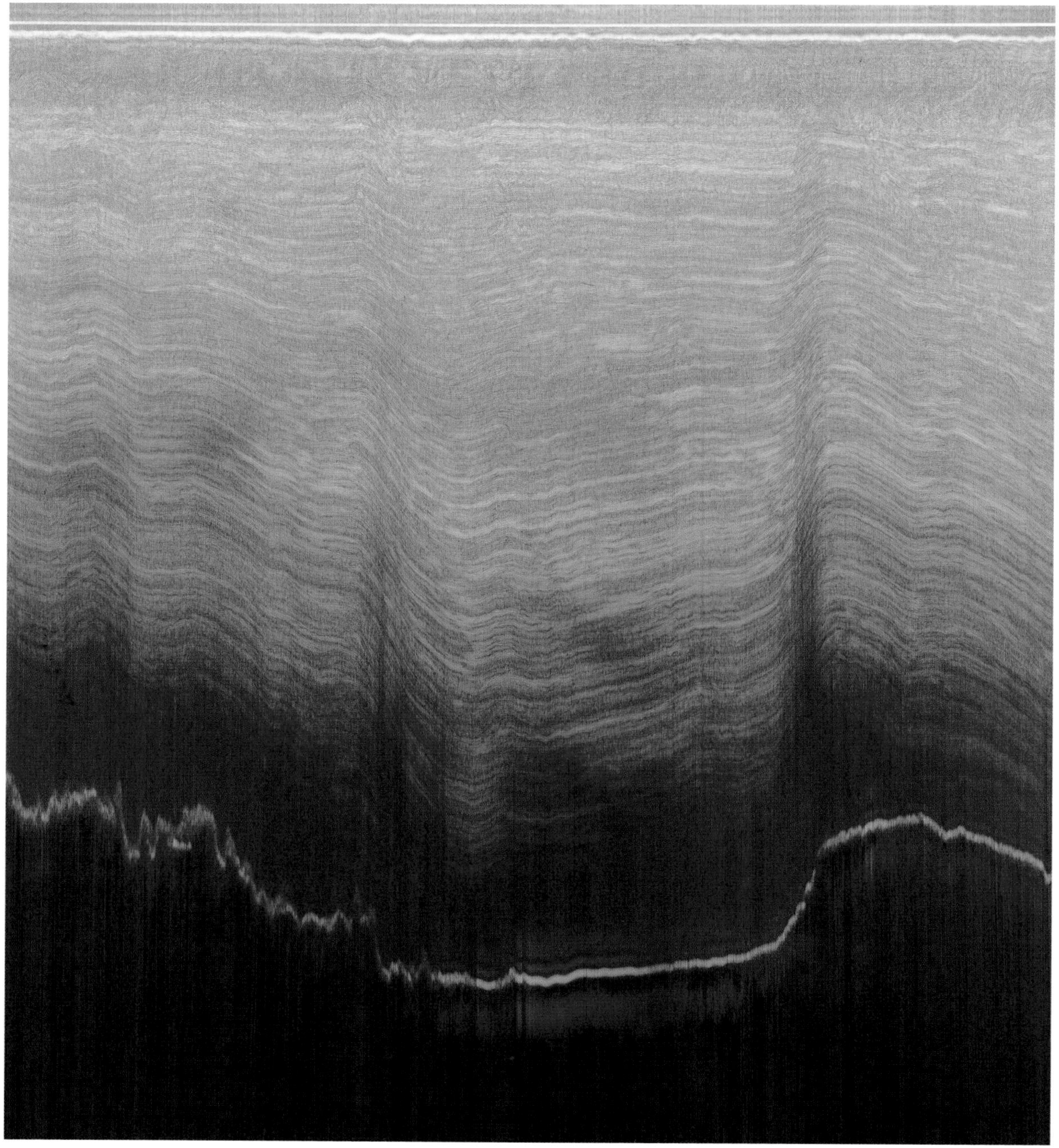

\+ **Lake Concordia,** From Flight W34, *2007,* Biro on an inkjet print on vinyl
\> + **Double Echo,** From Flight W38, *2007,* Inkjet print

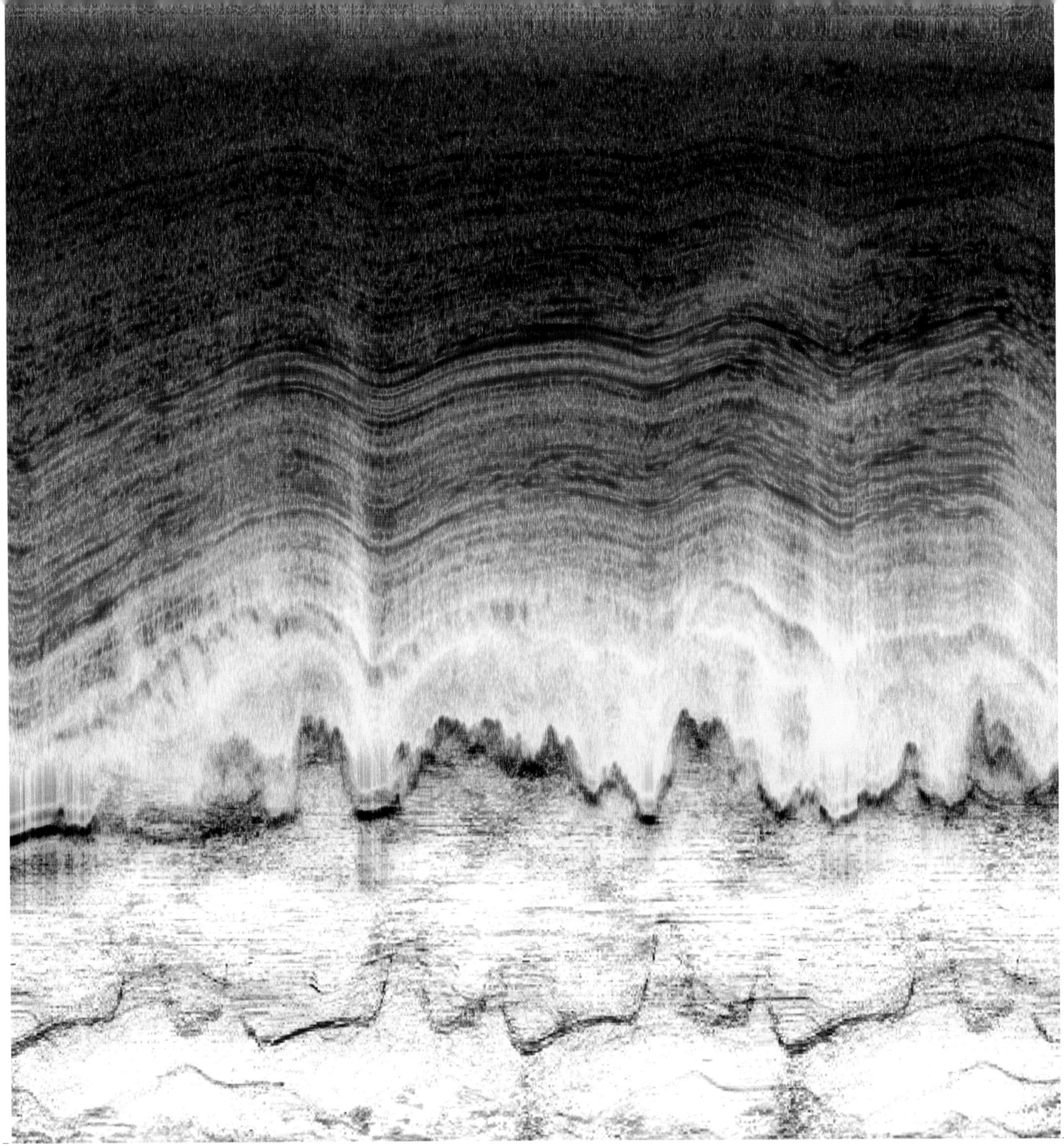

+ **Iceprint III,** Sky Blu, Antarctica, *2007,* Inkjet print
\> + **Albatross I,** *2007,* Inkjet print and pencil on artists' paper, courtesy British Antarctic Survey

Extract from blog

28th January 2007

When I first applied to come to Antarctica with BAS, my instinct was that I needed to experience one of the most extreme places on Earth, so it could act as a kind of benchmark of the macrocosm with which I could compare and link my findings in the microcosm: flow patterns and processes in the body. Having been here, I feel that instinct was right. I needed this experience to enter my very bones; to act as a baseline for further research.

The Antarctic ice cap is the place where global climate is born. It also stores, within its emptiness, the history of the last 900,000 years of the planet. The echo-recordings of the ice cap, which scientists out in the field are making by flying straight lines low over the ice cap with echo-sounding equipment attached to the undersides of the wings, give long computer drawings which are similar to echocardiogram readings of our hearts... glaciologists are trying to find ways of reading these echo-recorded drawings to give us an insight into the history of the planet. These drawings are like a heartbeat of Earth and ultimately that is where my interest as an artist lies.

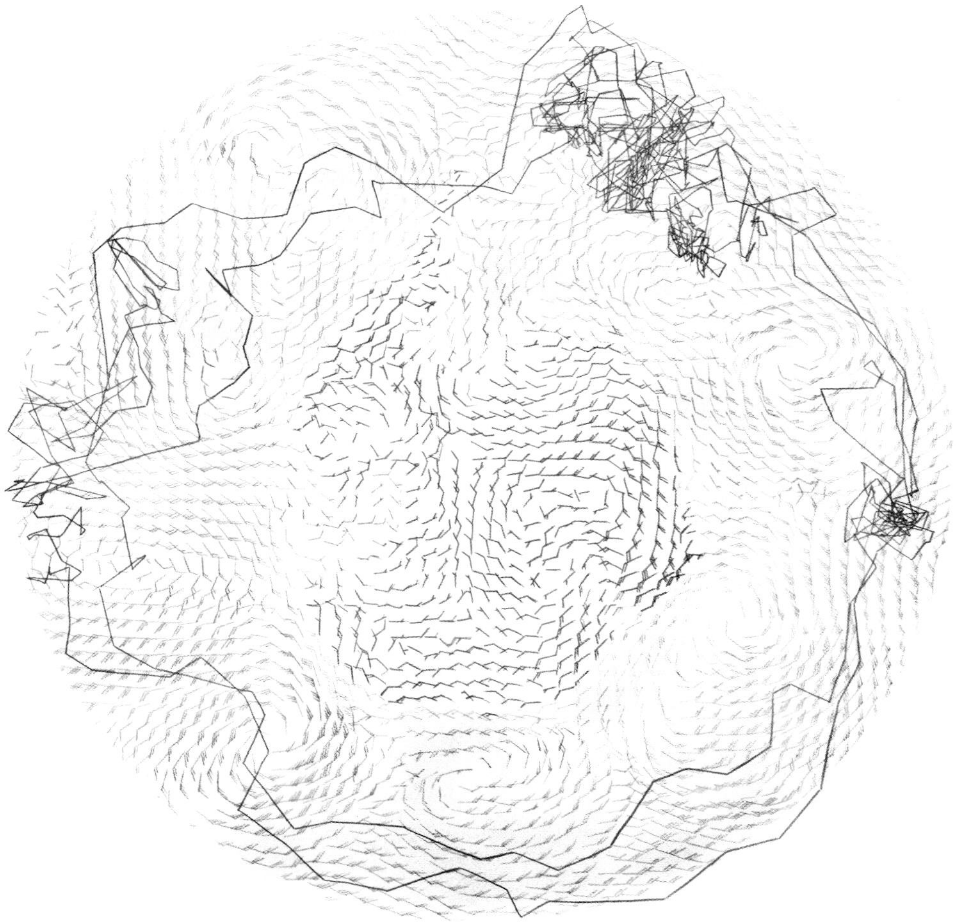

+ **Wind Vortices,** Sky Blu, Antarctica, *2007,* Inkjet print

CHRIS DRURY *(2006–2007)*

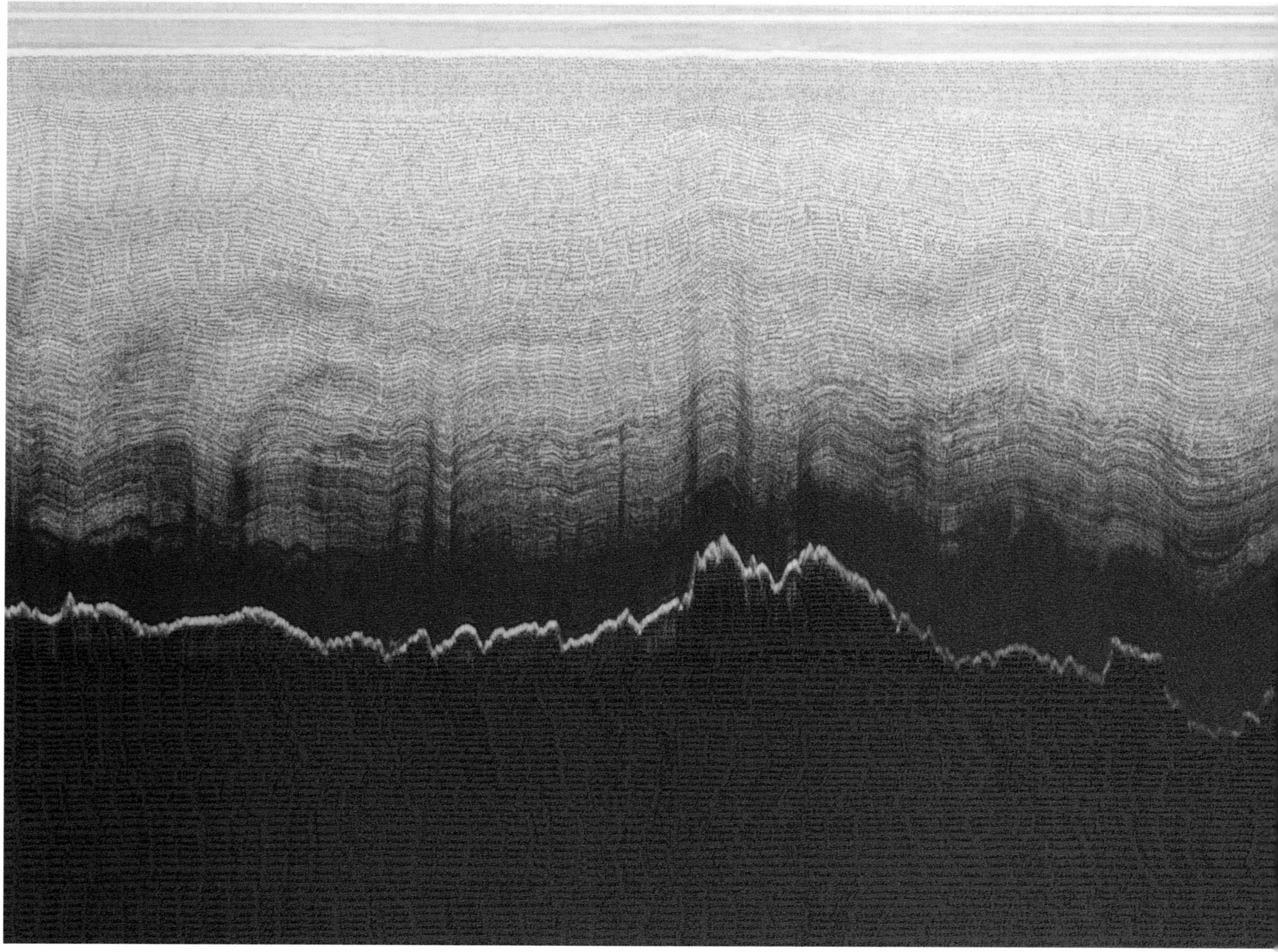

+ **Explorers at the Edge of the Void,** *2007,* Handwritten text in ink on an inkjet print from an echogram of East Antarctica, on artists' paper

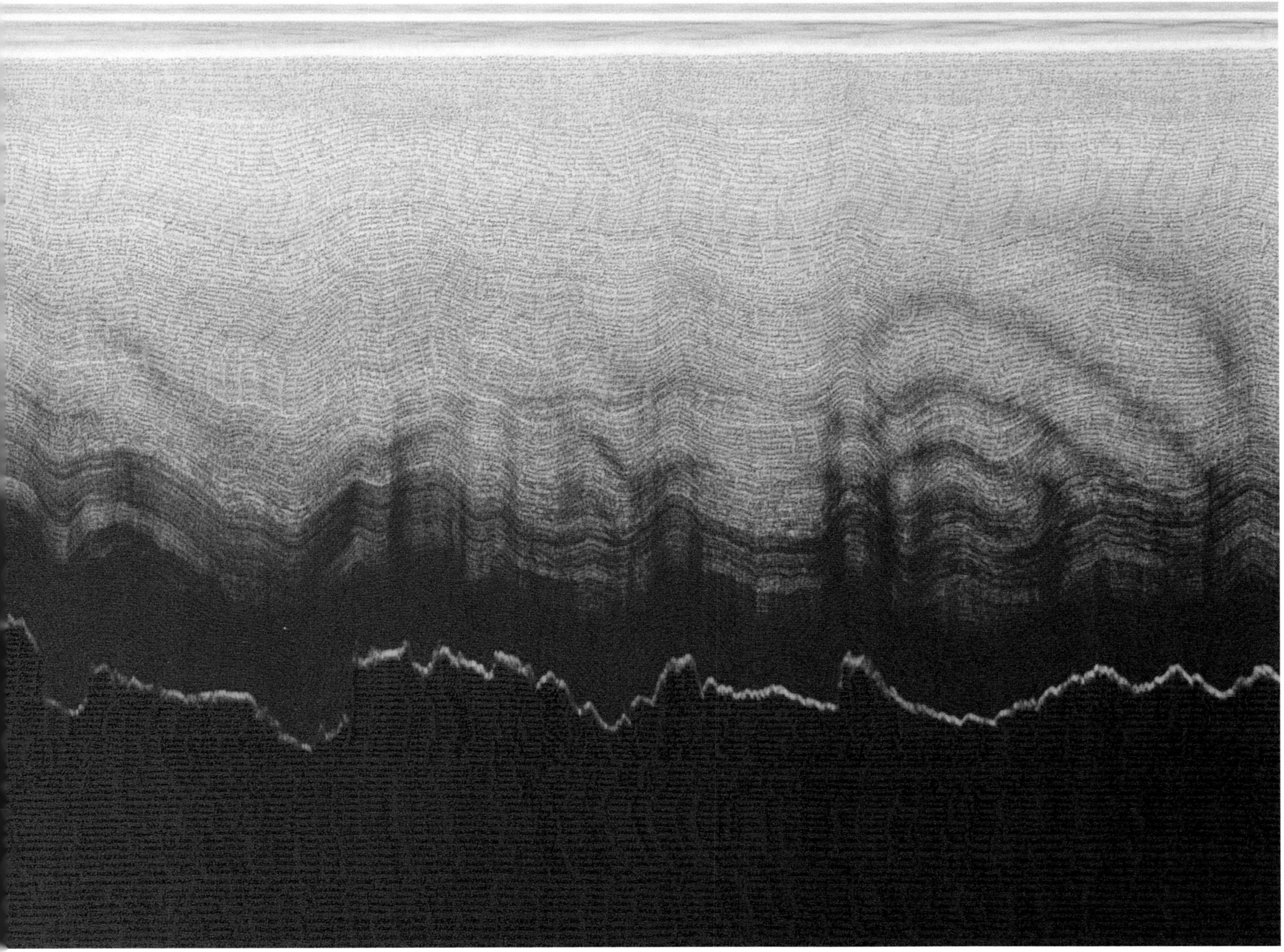

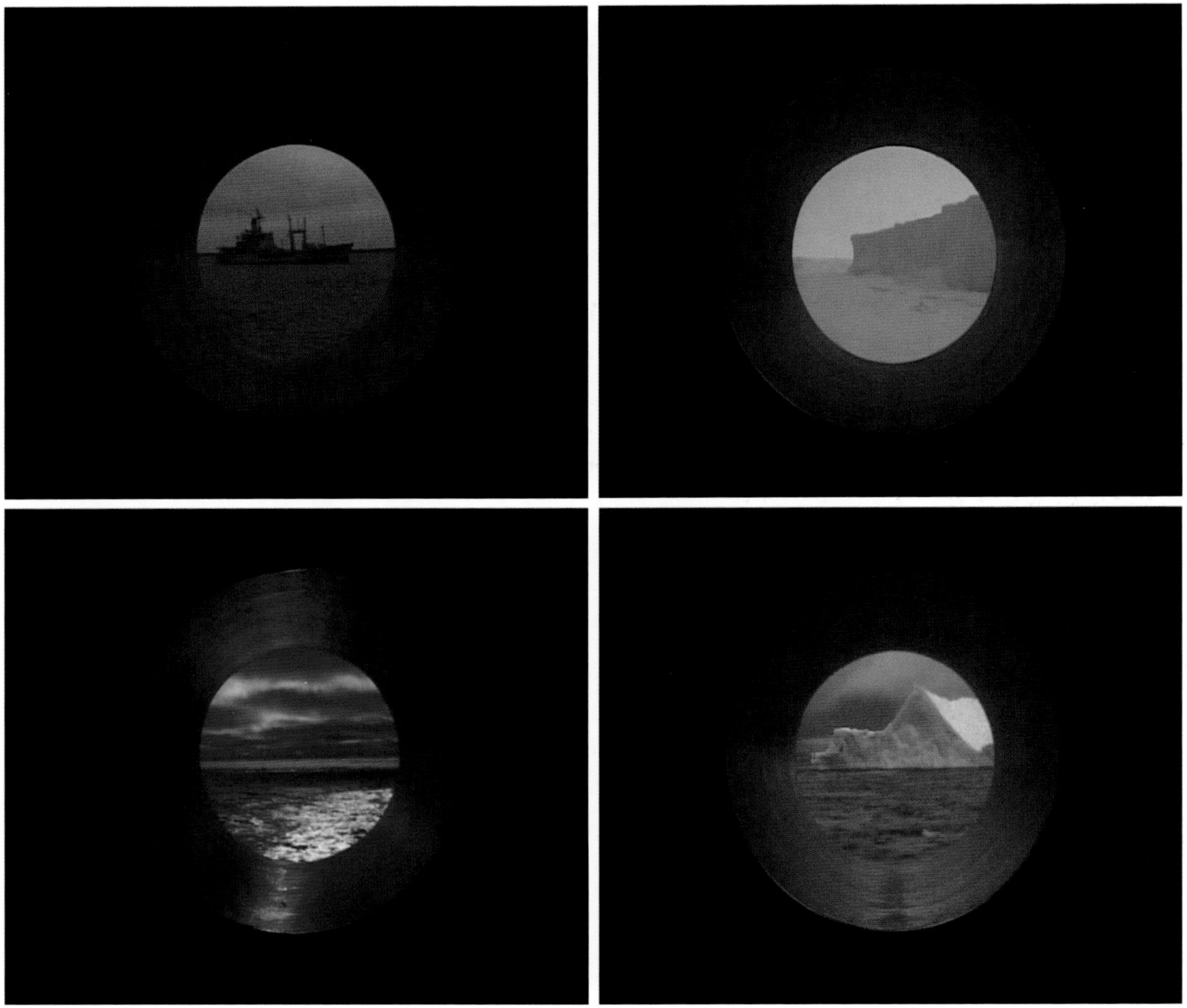

+ **44,** DVD, 44 mins, *2007,* Fourty-four pieces of footage from 44 days at sea
>+ **9/10ths,** *2005,* Digital photograph & digital drawing

1.
2.
3.
4.
5.
6.
7.
8.
9.

\+ We climbed round a final ridge and saw a whaling-boat entering the bay 2,500ft below.
A few moments later, we saw the sheds and factory of Stromness whaling-station.
We paused and shook hands — Ernest Shackleton, *2005,* DVD, 12 mins

+ **Escape Vehicle no.7,** *2005,* Two channel video, 7 mins + 1 min loop, On one monitor an orange suited figure disappears into the sky, on another the same figure is left flopping over the ice

< + Self Portrait - Halley Research Station, Antarctica, 12.05am, *2005,* Digital photograph
\+ Antarctica Dispatches (Drawing no.31: Halley Research Station, *2005,* Digital drawing dispatched by email

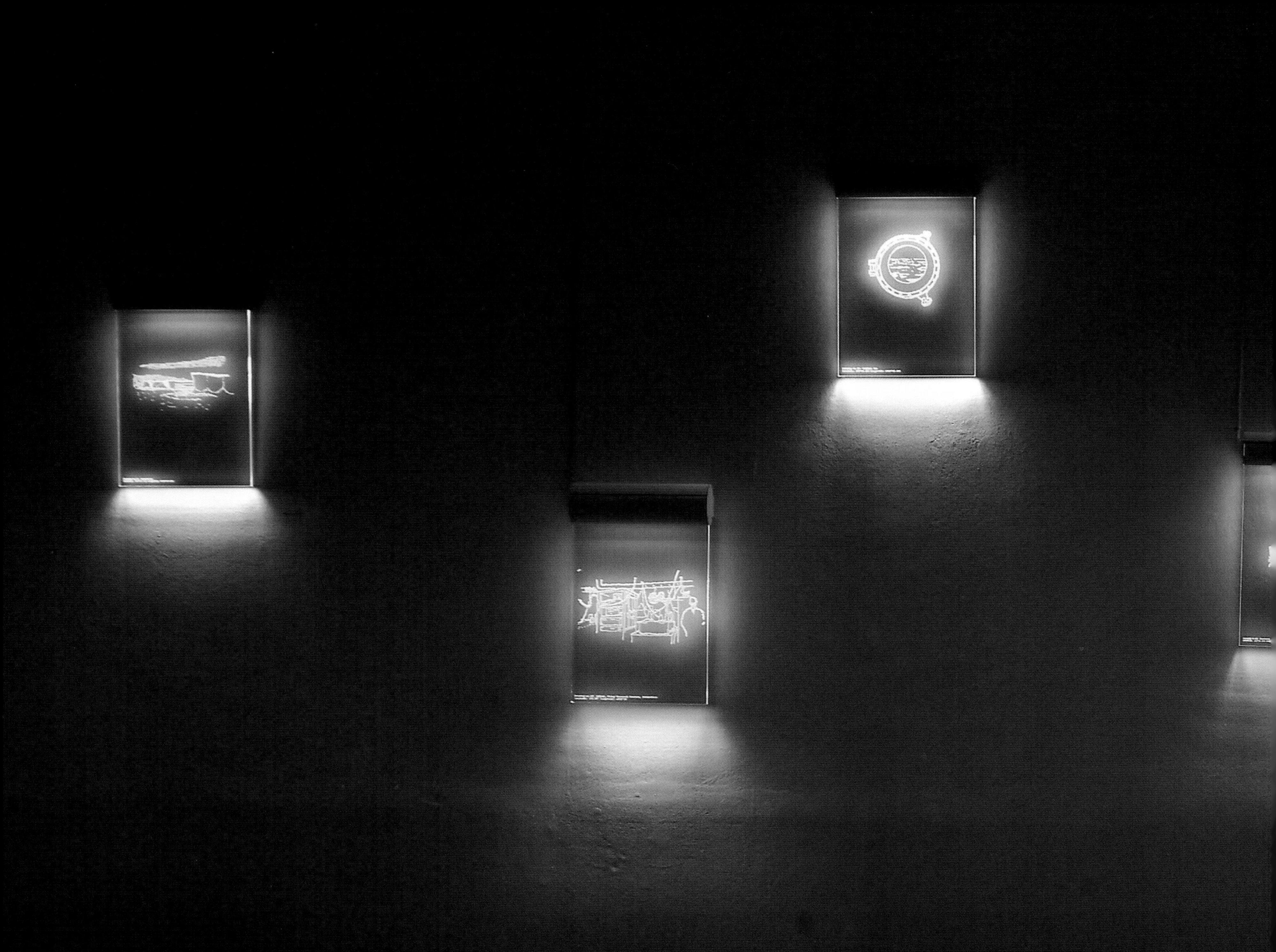

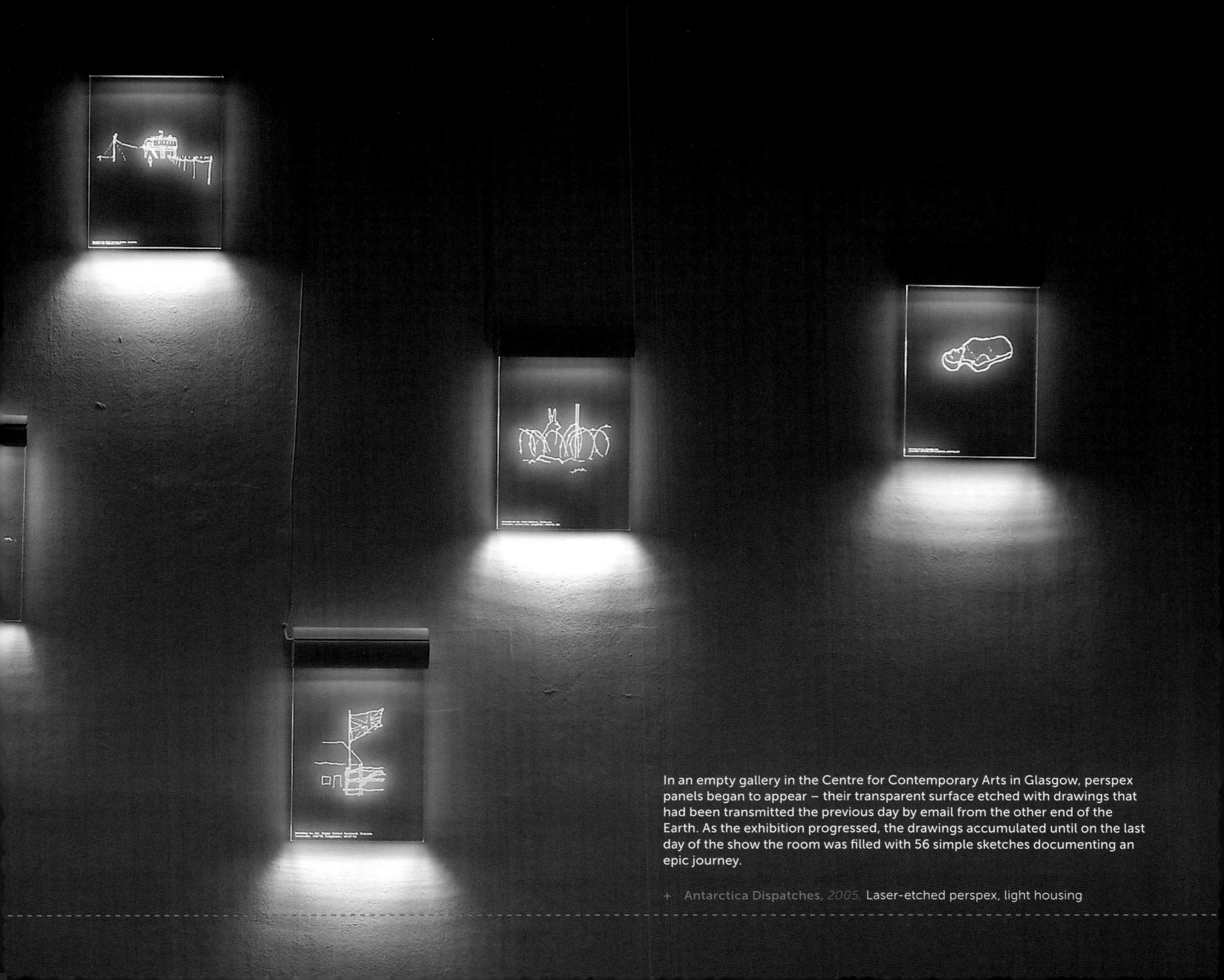

In an empty gallery in the Centre for Contemporary Arts in Glasgow, perspex panels began to appear – their transparent surface etched with drawings that had been transmitted the previous day by email from the other end of the Earth. As the exhibition progressed, the drawings accumulated until on the last day of the show the room was filled with 56 simple sketches documenting an epic journey.

+ Antarctica Dispatches, *2005,* Laser-etched perspex, light housing

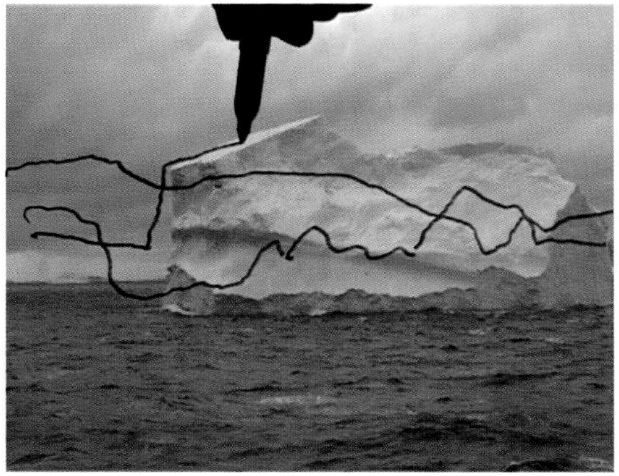

1st January 2009

Having finally broken through the pack ice late yesterday, we have been travelling along the shelf itself towards Halley. A 60m sheer face, which has been ripped and scoured, gouged out, collapsed, torn open with overhangs and undercuts. Cut by wind and sea like a piece of fabric caught on barbed wire in a gale.

But is also stunningly beautiful, so 'other' and unreal. A place where scale and perspective are unreliable guides. Even when you are right up close it seems so ephemeral, and insubstantial.

+ **In Transit**, *2008–2009,* Stills from video work drawing on the Bridge windows of the *Ernest Shackleton* on our journey to and from Halley

27th January 2009

Last night I took out my kite. The sun was bright with a wind of about seven knots which was coming directly from the west. To fly it, I walked straight into the sun. It was cold, about minus seven, but perfect for flying. Amazingly, within half an hour, the wind turned through 180 degrees and was suddenly coming directly from the east. The temperature dropped to minus 17 degrees and a bright mist appeared in moments. Then a very strange thing – 'diamond dust' filled my vision. Very tiny slithers of ice blowing and floating through the air and reflecting the light like its description, a shower of vanishing diamonds...

9th February 2009

You probably don't remember, but an enduring memory I have is of the first ever moon landing. I seem to remember that day in South Africa, everyone looking upwards just waiting for Apollo 11 to pass overhead. Now that appears fanciful but that's how I picture the afternoon. If you don't recall the day you will remember Neil Armstrong's first words "That's one small step for man, one giant leap for mankind" and the image of the flag being planted in front of the strange, four-legged landing capsule.

The Halley base is equally strange on its legs, equally a product of science fiction, its location every bit as bereft of life or visual interest as the surface of the moon. Above the front entrance, on a tall mast the Union Jack is flapping. Each year a new flag is raised in mid-August on the day the sun makes its first appearance, labouring over the horizon and heralding the end of winter. The current one is torn, shredded into four or five long frayed ribbons from being whipped by the wind for the past six months. There are also lines of flags across the landscape, little black or red squares of cloth on bamboo canes, part buried, some bent double, all shredded. Flags which mark the terrain, safe routes or dangerous locations... The little lines of bamboo canes look so pathetic, so completely insignificant stretching out a few miles into the distance over a continent. All you can hope is that our ingenuity and greed are never so great that it can tame or destroy what is here.

+ **P1(t) = p1(0) + [p1(t1) – p1(0)] t/t1,** *2009,* One cubic metre of ice relocated 100m and reburied

12th February 2009

The temperature is hovering at around minus 12–14 during the day, but as dusk approaches it is easily the wrong side of minus 20. Last night, I went down to the cliffs overlooking the sea to fly my kite. The sky was clear with the sun hovering just above the Earth and the sea beginning to freeze. Its surface was covered with a thick gluey layer of 'grease ice', and where there was still open water, it undulated like viscous black oil. A thin layer of mist was rolling off the shelf and rising over the water as the very cold air met with the slightly warmer water. In the bay, close to the edge of the ice, there was a large pod of killer whales, the only audible sound the regular whoosh as they expelled plumes of air. When the ice coagulates it forms solid discs, 'biscuit ice' which itself gradually merges together into an impenetrable fortress of sea ice...

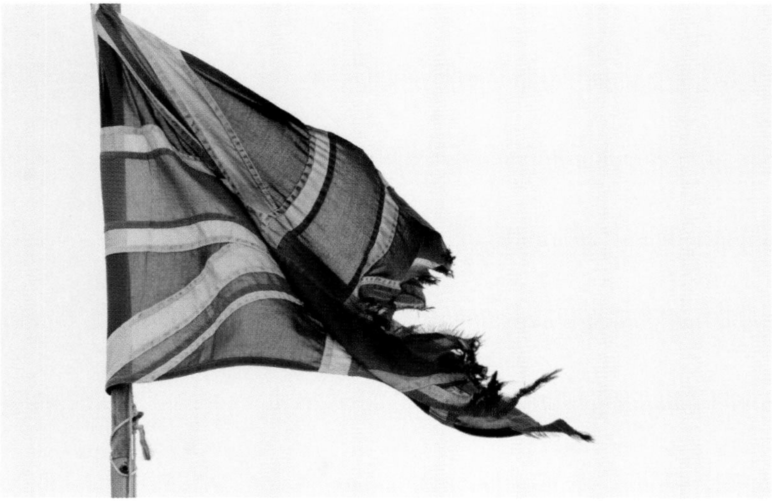

+ Halley Station

+ **Wide-eyed and legless – Antarctica,** *2009,* Video installation using images of Antarctica filmed using a kite

+ **Small Albatross,** *2004,* Oil on canvas

\+ **Icebergs and Moon,** *2008,* Oil on canvas

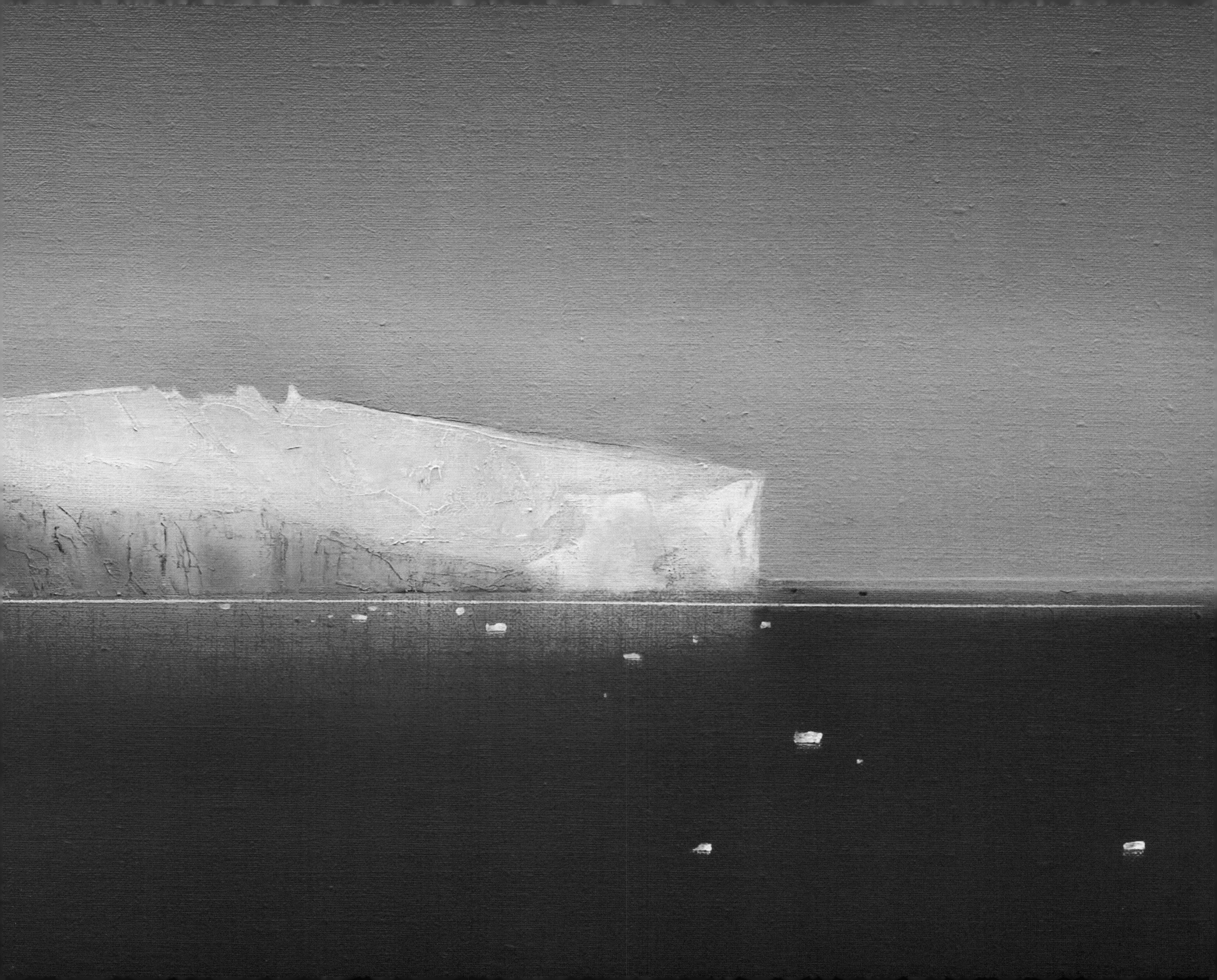

Journal extracts from
On Royal Research Ship, *James Clark Ross*

20th November 2001

I have made my first drawings – hopelessly inadequate to show anything of the power and majesty of these seas. The light is radiant but with an intensity beyond my previous experience. The sea is transmuted into quicksilver in a broad avenue of scintillating light beneath the high sun. Literally it is as if the sea is of mercury. I can only think of silver leaf as a way of representing it. On the horizon, which is blurred, rests a broad band of cloud, which extends upwards creating an enormous frieze of luminous mist. The clouds above this band of mist are high ribbons of stratus breaking into horizontal bands interspaced with a light-suffused pale grey/blue.Below, the incessant turmoil is of a counter-change between the huge swell and the smaller waves born within it. The detailing of the sweeping rhythms – the high riding crests and the glassy mirror-like surfaces all speeding along with the ship and divided and inscribed by the trajectories of the gliding aerodynamic gulls. We are under a transparent bell of light upon which the wind's breath condenses causing effects of pale translucency.

25th November 2001 – Off Elephant Island

My first view of Antarctica is breathtaking. The power and the weight of it – the geometrical sky – fixing by a loose co-ordinate of clouds a spatial perspective which is mirrored on the sea. The colour is of the widest variety and harmony and the tones are rich and sonorous. Deep brown purples contrasting with orange/yellow cloudlets brightly illuminated by an invisible sun. Intense beams of light outline in brilliance the cracks and protuberances in the deep ice and snow of the islands.

Here are mountains under monstrous weights of ice – and isolated rocks which rise vertically from the sea – in surreal majesty clothed in a warm glow of reflected light. Mighty walls – unscaleable – remote and imponderable in their immanence of being. The astonishing relationships of the elements in this first glimpse of the vastness which in several days from now I will be entering, is bewildering in its magnificence. It almost defeats this artist before he has begun.

26th November 2001

I have made several drawings of the ocean juggling with the tilting planes of the sea. Planes which break into furiously boiling crests of foam arising from a sheen of the most lovely turquoise blue/green. The hollows between the tremendous seas are almost alarmingly deep and sometimes the wave crests hover above the stern and to each side of it.

< + **Iceberg off Rothera Point,** *2006,* Oil on canvas

+ **A Nameless Place,** *2007,* Oil on canvas

At Rothera

9th December 2001

Islands of ice, mountains encrusted with driven snow – the dry rock scoured by the abrasive wind – the entire land area a compacted wilderness of white. The sea crowded by green and blue glass flotillas of icebergs. The wind from the north with its intimation of home – voices strung along the lines of air – dear voices – warm and comforting though borne on an indifferent gale.

At Fossil Bluff

11th December 2001

This morning I walked from the landing ski–way back to the base – almost a kilometer and a half. I stopped frequently – at one time snow began to fall but a snow of such softness and peace, the individual flakes floating down from a patch of blue, a lagoon within encircling cloud. The sun illuminated each flake which descended past the deep black-brown gravel slopes of the nearby mountain wall. It was a momentary experience of the purest poetry and mood.

Later I stopped walking and was at once aware of the physical sensation of silence quite beyond normal conception. I do not think I will know a stillness of such transcendental power this side of my death. The beating of my heart was the only sound as I stood motionless breathing softly. Then I was aware of the presence of a continuous near-imperceptible hiss. It reminded me of the background radiation of the Universe – a 'static' on the sensory receive of my brain. I could not decide if the sound came from within my head or was indeed the almost inaudible sound of the vast snow and ice fields which stretched to the blurred horizon. A subdued light was unevenly reflected from the plains before me. A shaft of brilliance like the blade of a gigantic fallen sword separated the two horizontal halves of the distance upon which chains of mountains seemed to be dissolving into pale banks of mist. The subtle, insinuating sound continued in the faintest of sustained whispering. Something inarguable touched my imagination – I seemed suspended between life, time and death – there was no history, simply the presence of the eternal existence of nature. More than the dramatic phenomena of Antarctica, the insistent appeal of its mystery through a voice in the lowest audible register possible will remain in my consciousness.

A problem for me in painting, based on these southern field experiences, will be to express the apparent emptiness and vacancy of these landscapes while yet being able to allude to the enormous distances involved.

+ **Silence, Antarctica,** *2007,* Oil on canvas

Artist Statement

Together with Keith Grant, I was the first artist to go to Antarctica on the BAS Artists and Writers Programme, from November 2001–January 2002.

My normal way of working is to walk and draw in the landscape and then do all the painting back at the studio. So Antarctica did not represent any marked change in my working methods – except more extreme conditions and the 24-hour day, which meant there was never any reason to stop working. I did no painting on the ship and back in the base, but did do quite a lot of processing of digital photographs and selective printing that entered into my notebooks.

On return to England, I produced a series of paintings that were exhibited in Australia and England. I drew so much that even 10 years later there is still work available to develop. For me, the whole period was like no other. The images remain.

One unexpected benefit was the welcome in the communities, both on the ship and at the research station. One soon becomes close friends. The normal life of an artist is lonely – this was a wonderful exception.

Philip Hughes, September 2011

\+ **Mount Carrara,** *2002,* Aquacryl & gouache on paper, 67 x 101cm

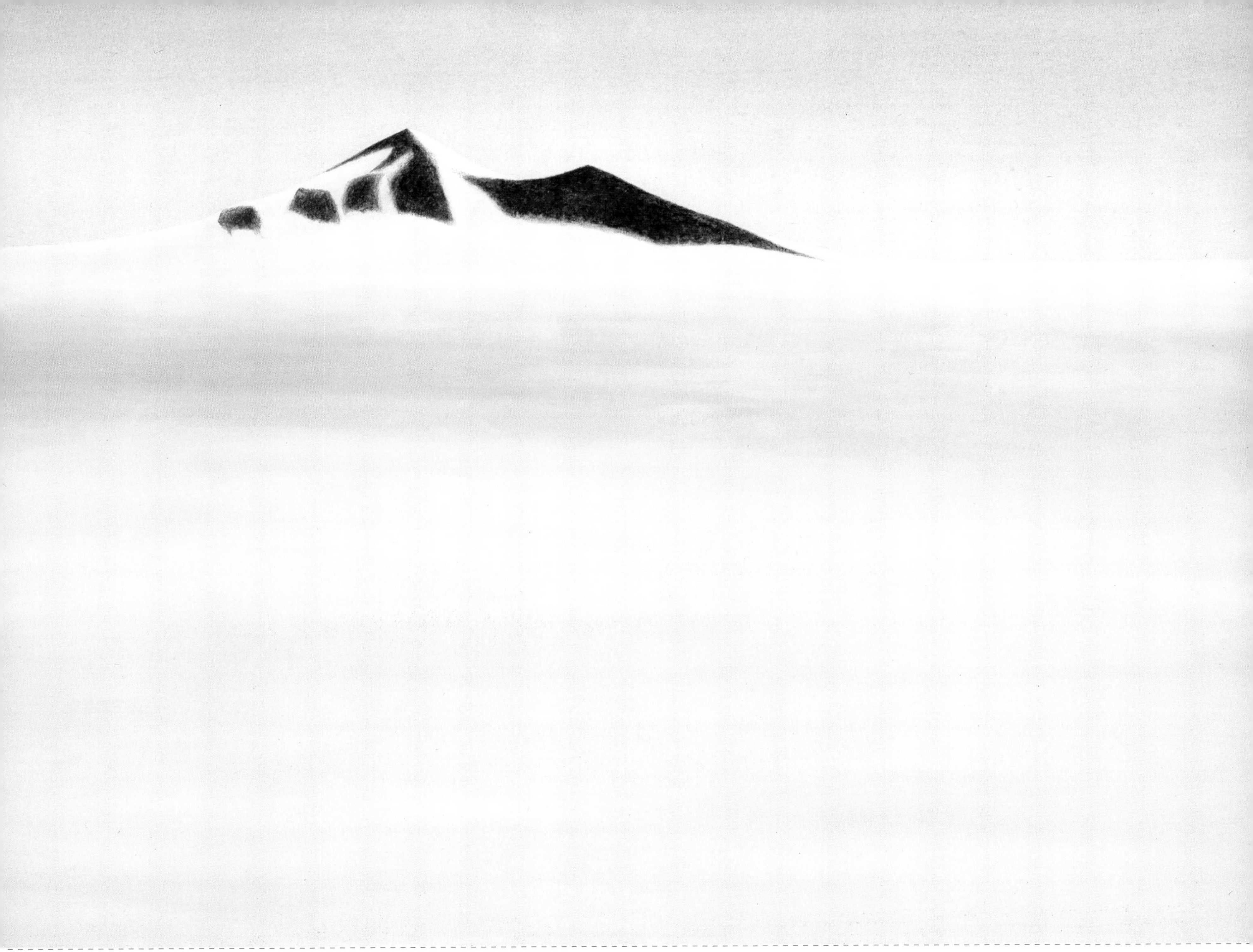

+ **Above Sky Blu,** *2003,* Acrylic on canvas, 80 x 80cm

+ **Nunataks at Sky Blu,** *2003,* Acrylic on canvas, 80 x 140cm

Excerpts from diary
November 2001 – January 2002

My seven-week stay started with a two-week voyage on the research ship from the Falklands to the research base at Rothera.

Saturday 24th November
8.30pm The first sight of Antarctica. Elephant Island, where Shackleton's men were stranded. Awesome looking, sheer peaks, black with huge glaciers. We turn here and go back to Drake's Passage but it is a foretaste!

Sunday 25th November (Francesca's Birthday)
Got up at 3am to see Elephant Island at its closest. This is the first sight of Antarctica and intensely exciting. Do first drawing/sketch of landscape. New birds – white-headed petrel and southern fulmar.

Sunday 2nd December
8.00pm Drinking in the Captain's cabin after dinner. Robert, the mate, puts head around door to say that ice is carrying us at 1 knot towards reefs. So quick break up from this surreal comfort. Engines at maximum power we edge so slowly forward away from the ice trap. Even at full power we were barely moving. Doubts creep in on how soon we shall get through.

Tuesday 4th December
Later – we cut to the north, then across and take a route SE quite close to islands and reefs. And we get through. Fantastic ice trip with large flows and icebergs.

Arrival at Rothera more spectacular than I imagined.
6.00pm tie up!

Friday 14th December
2.30pm Weather, if anything worse. I went for a walk if you could call it that, a stagger in Force 10/11 with snow. Was blown over. This is quite something. If I am right even the Met man is in awe.

Saturday 15th December
But – miraculously as we flew on to Sky Blu it cleared, and there was a wonderful view of the Nunataks sticking up above the ice cap. As we landed at last I felt I had really arrived in Antarctica. As the evening progressed, the sky cleared and finally I saw the real midnight sun quite high above the horizon and with ice and snow all around, brilliant light.

Monday 17th December
7.00pm As the evening went on, I discovered why it was blue ice where I was sitting. The wind swept down from the mountain above. It was seriously cold as the wind rose. On return to base, I was feeling really exposed. The thermometer said -16°C but the wind chill made it far colder.

Friday 21st December (Midsummer Day)
8.20am Leave to fly to Larsen Ice Shelf to service an automatic weather station. Although not as brilliant as the day before, another 1¼ hour flight there full of dramatic/fabulous land. Mountains with vast glaciers. Then we reach the seemingly endless ice shelf. We hunt around for this speck, a small tower with box attached. After one false landing, Nick spots it.

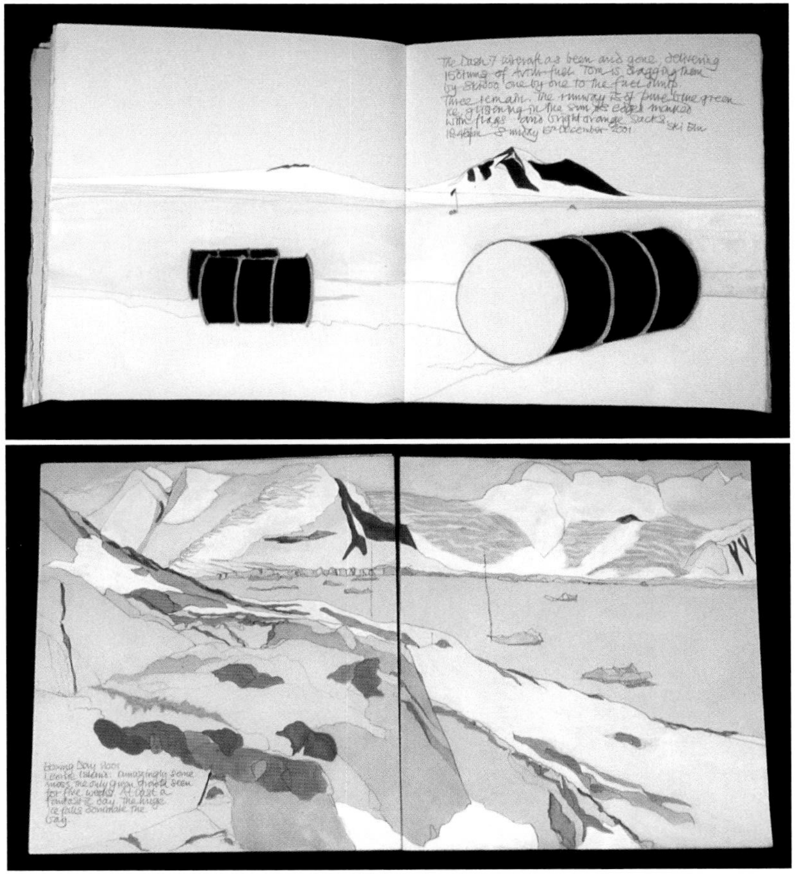

Sunday 23rd December
Wow. A heavy night at the bar – with a sort of disco thrown in. The three women dancing plus a couple of men dressed as women. Well, with such a ratio of M to F one has to be imaginative.

I go and draw again at the end of the runway. Trying to finish multipart image of the ice cliff. To my amazement, the view has changed since Saturday. There has been a huge icefall with a large part of the cliff now in the sea. And as I was drawing another large fall sent a sort of tidal wave through the bay, all the drift ice shaking and rattling. I had the usual company of penguins and a seal swimming. I watched with fascination as a penguin clambered up a nearby iceberg and then set off on a series of toboggan runs down its slopes.

Monday 31st December (New Year's Eve)
Yesterday's fabulous balmy calm replaced by traditional wind from the north. Nevertheless, Adam and I continue with plans to climb Reptile Ridge. It starts with an hour's rope training. Then off. We climb ramp and at top rope up, crampons etc. and climb the ice ridges. Fantastic (again!) though hard work and extremely difficult to draw and photograph in high wind blowing a gale with gusts even more. Leave at 10. Back at 16.00.

Rest a bit.
Then New Year's Eve.

Two bands and disco in the transformed garage workshop. A lot of crazy dancing – still only five women but dancing not reduced. At midnight, great greetings of everyone. I have not seen such closeness of a group ever. Moving, in a way.
Finally bed at 2.00 plus.

+ **Notebook volumes 3 & 4**, *2001*, Mixed media on paper, 29 x 33cm (closed)

\+ **The camp at Sky Blu,** *2003,* Acrylic on canvas, 164 x 226cm

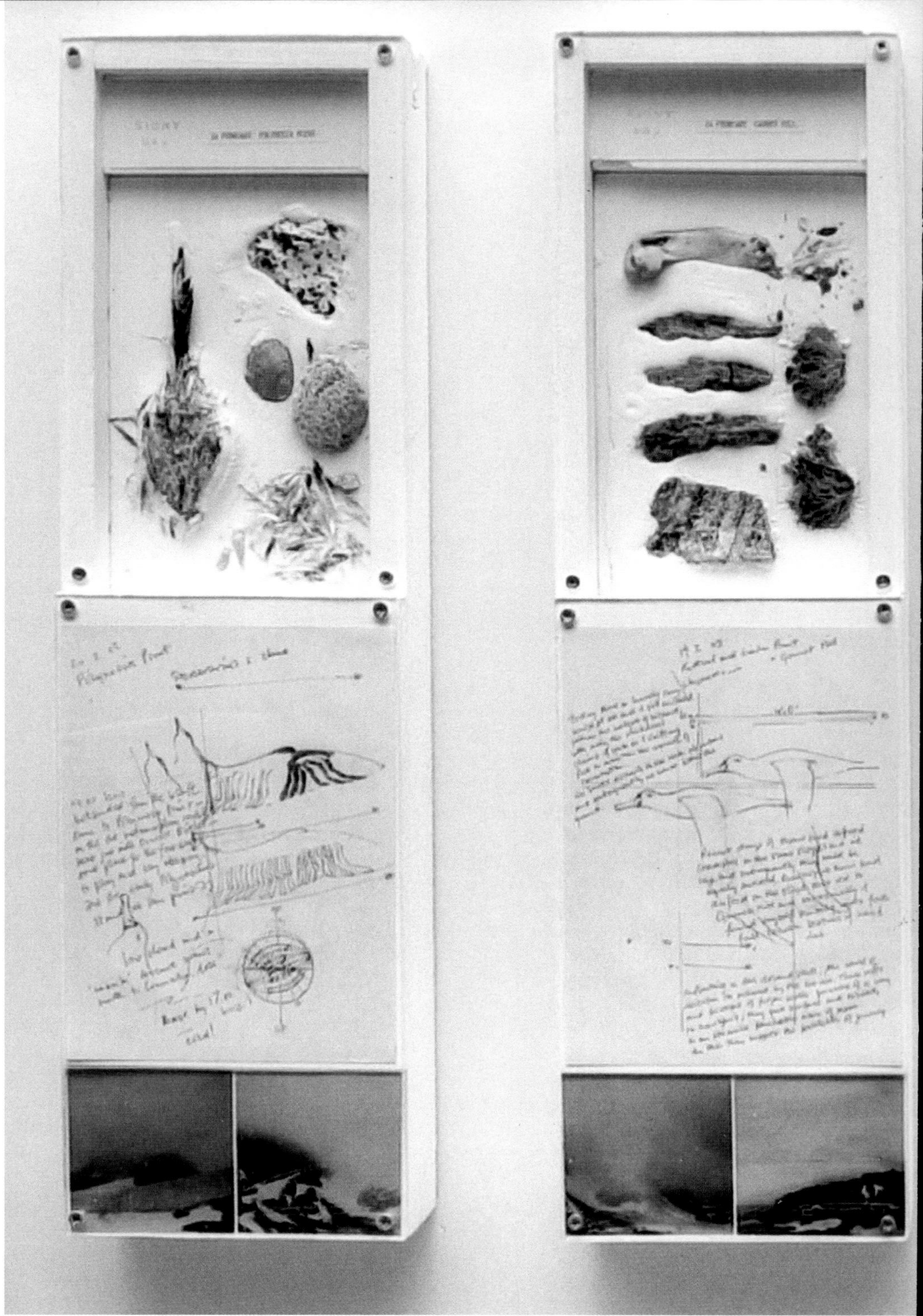

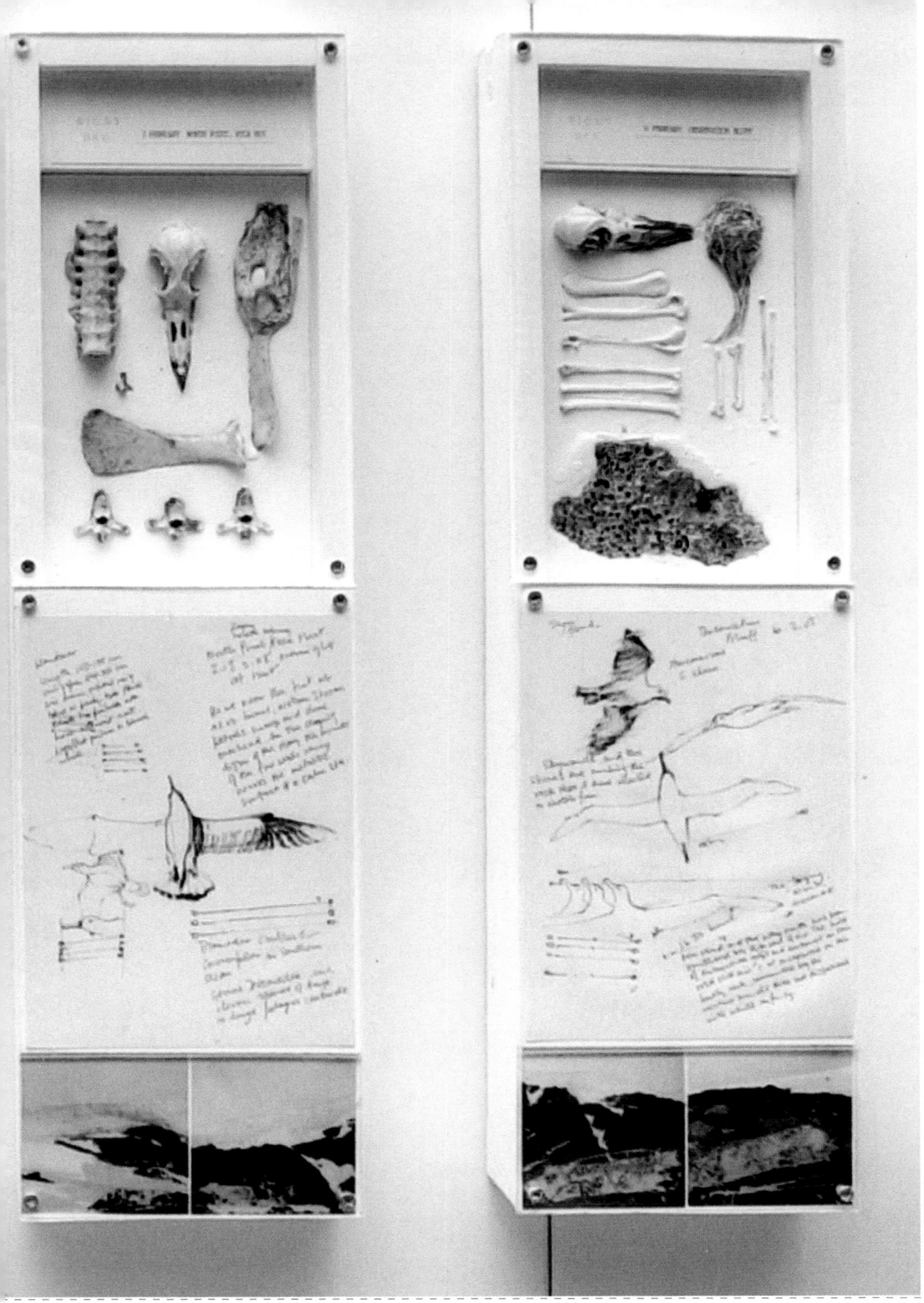

+ **Southern Forensics (24),** *2003,* Photographs, drawings, bone, feather, rock and plaster, 21″ x 6″ x 3″

The journey to Antarctica and my subsequent travels within the northern polar area have established an approach to landscape that allows for the input of both science and personal reflection. It is a combination that has opened new perspectives on the complex systems that constantly affect our planet. Consequently, working methods and the range of work now embrace the broader issues of climatic and environmental change.

Extract from journal
Southern Ocean

22nd January 2003

Almost by chance,
A glance to port
And there
The effortless glide
On wings too slender

And later that day,

In low flight,
the occasional motion of wings.
Close to the ocean skin
The great bird passes
Over the slate grey water.

Extracts from journal
Due South

Days at Sea — 24th January 2003

I awake to a grey overcast day with variable wind and a slight swell. In the haze of early morning the silver grey outline of the first iceberg appears in the cold light of mid-distance. This spectre, so full of weighty omen, causes unfamiliar thoughts to pass through my mind.

Signy Island Journal — 15th February 2003

In Antarctica the light of the blank surface is thrown back at you. It reflects upon you, causing introspection. The eye-mind cannot register upon movement or depth of colour; it has to contend with a nothingness, an infinity. It is the intimidation of a white canvas and the fear of a blank page.

5th March 2003

Standing at Robin Peak the silence is absolute and sufficient to hear a whale's breath. Only the low thunder of avalanche and the explosive crack of ice collapse enter the still air for fleeting moments. To the west, through near perfect visibility, spreads the dramatic expanse of the sea ice. Somewhere within the still grey waters, whales swim amid the avenues of ice and the opaline surfaces of the shelves, beneath expectant air, the sheen of the ocean skin and the depths of the blue world of suspended ice.

7th March 2003

10.00 hrs
The *RRS Ernest Shackleton* arrives and dispatches a small craft that threads its way through the ice to deliver two personnel and to pick up the four who are leaving. Once we have secured our lifebelts and jackets we are off, and skim over a rough sea into the snowstorm. Salt water and ice crystals strike my face, and by the time we pull alongside of the ship, my hands are frozen to a bright red and blue patchwork.

19:00 hrs
Making my way to the upper deck, I look towards Signy and can still make out a dark shape through the gloom. As night descends, so the beams of light from the ship illuminate the immediate waters as we move on and manoeuvre our passage through the icebergs. I look at the great walls of ice drifting within the grey waters and realise that Signy has now gone from view and disappeared into the cold black distance of the polar night.

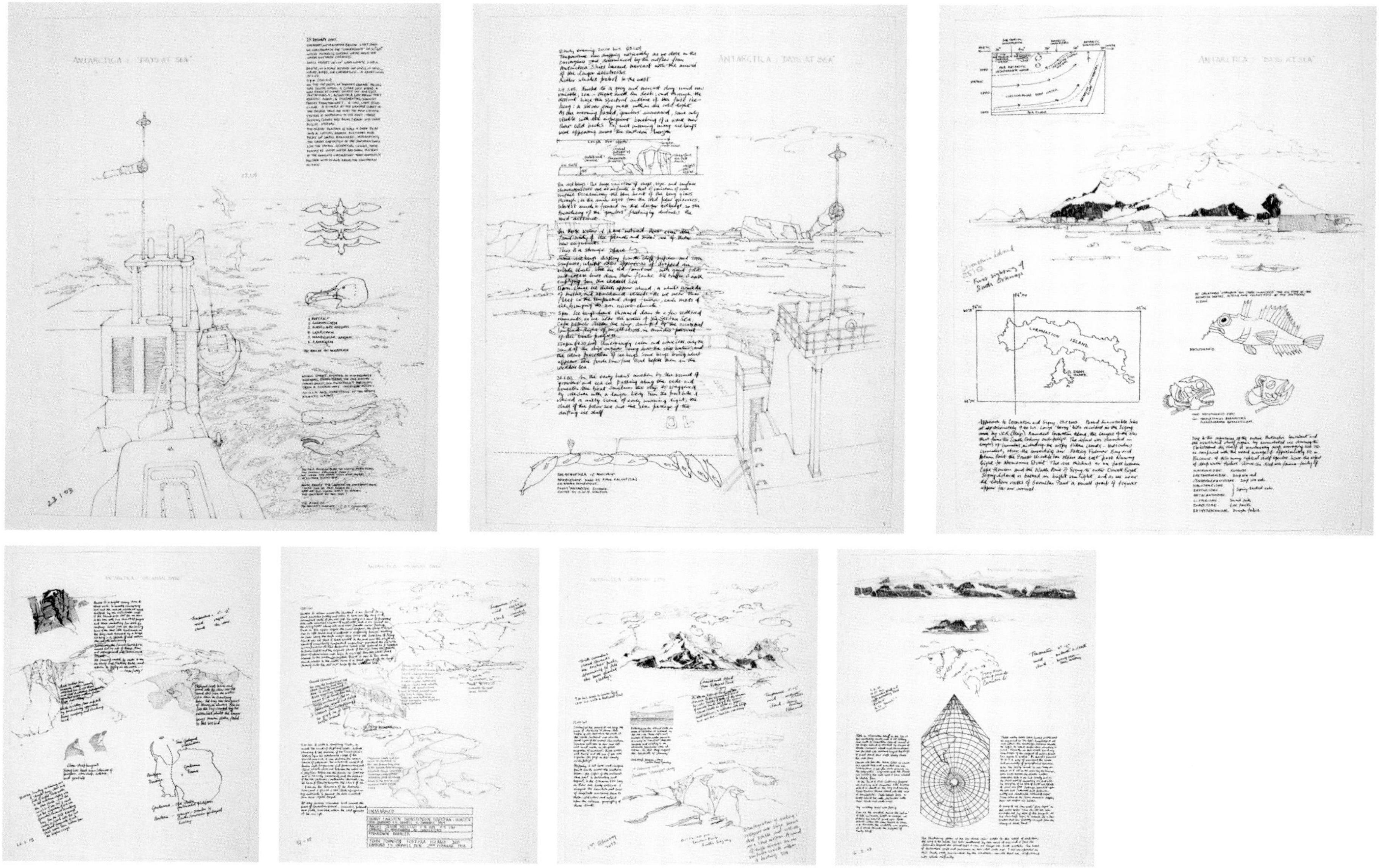

+ **Visual Diaries (24),** *2003,* Pen, pencil and ink, 18" x 14" (33" x 23" frame size)

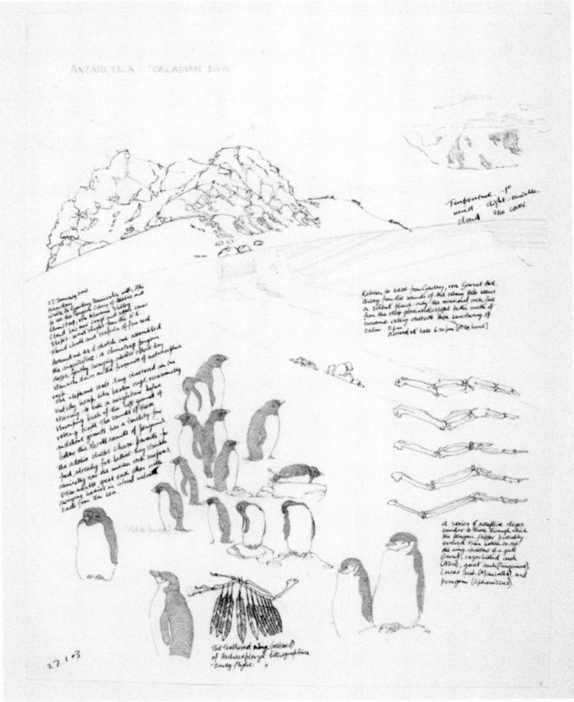

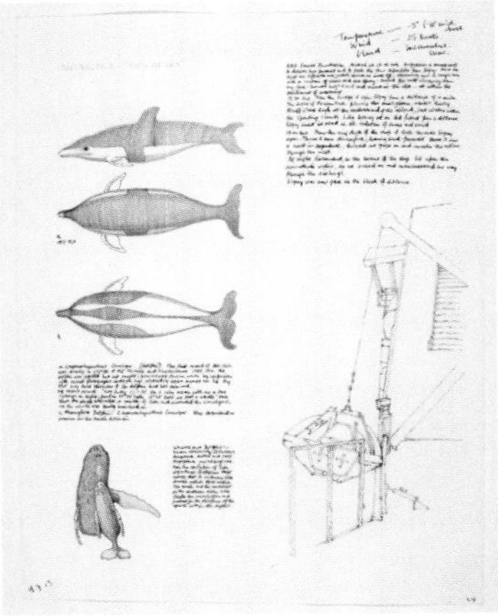

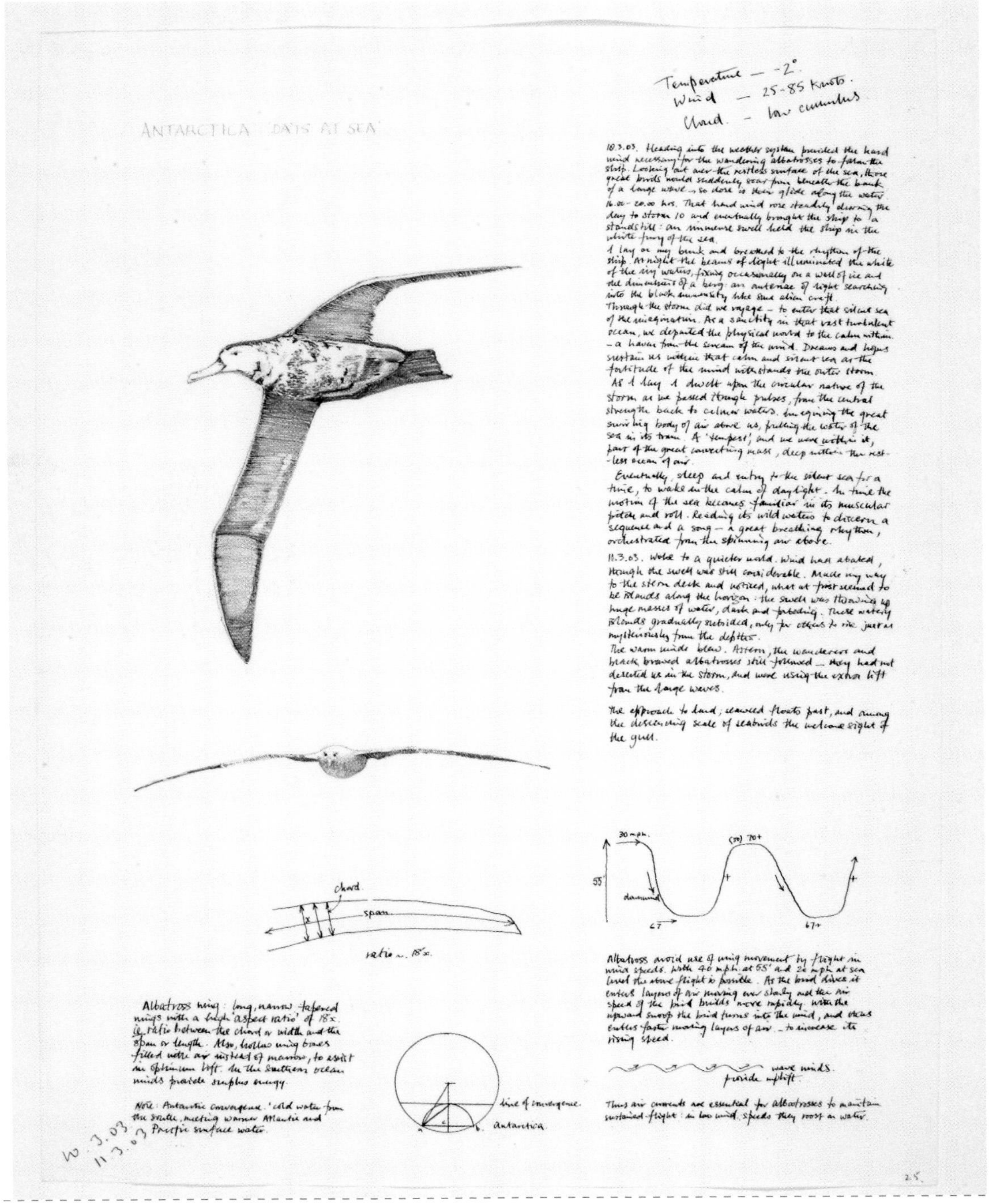
ANTARCTICA 'DAYS AT SEA'
Temperature — -2°
Wind — 25-85 knots.
Cloud. — low cumulus
10.3.03. Heading into the weather system provided the hard wind necessary for the wandering albatrosses to follow the ship. Looking out over the restless surface of the sea, those great birds would suddenly soar from beneath the bank of a large wave, so close is their glide along the water.
16.00 - 20.00 hrs. That hard wind rose steadily during the day to storm 10 and eventually brought the ship to a standstill: an immense swell held the ship in the white fury of the sea.
I lay on my bunk and breathed to the rhythm of the ship. At night the beams of light illuminated the white of the icy waters, fixing occasionally on a wall of ice and the dimensions of a berg: an antennae of light searching into the black immensity like some alien craft.
Through the storm did we voyage – to enter that silent sea of the imagination. As a sanctity in that vast turbulent ocean, we departed the physical world to the calm within – a haven from the scream of the wind. Dreams and hopes sustain us within that calm and silent sea as the fortitude of the mind withstands the outer storm.
As I lay I dwelt upon the circular nature of the storm as we passed through pulses, from the central strength back to calmer waters. Imagining the great swirling body of air above us, pulling the water of the sea in its train. A 'tempest', and we were within it, part of the great convecting mass, deep within the restless ocean of air.
Eventually, sleep and entry to the silent sea for a time, to wake in the calm of daylight. In time the motion of the sea becomes familiar in its muscular pitch and roll. Reading its wild waters to discern a sequence and a song – a great breathing rhythm, orchestrated from the spinning air above.
11.3.03. Woke to a quieter world. Wind had abated, though the swell was still considerable. Made my way to the stern deck and noticed, what at first seemed to be islands along the horizon: the swell was throwing up huge masses of water, dark and foreboding. These watery islands gradually subsided, only for others to rise just as mysteriously from the depths.
The warm winds blew. Astern, the wanderers and black browed albatrosses still followed – they had not deserted us in the storm, and were using the extra lift from the large waves.
The approach to land; seaweed floats past, and among the descending scale of seabirds the welcome sight of the gull.
chord.
span.
ratio ~ 18x.
30 mph.
(70) 70+
55'
downwind
67
67+
Albatross wing: long, narrow tapered wings with a high 'aspect ratio' of 18x. ie ratio between the chord or width and the span or length. Also, hollow wing bones filled with air instead of marrow, to assist in optimum lift. In the Southern ocean winds provide surplus energy.
Albatross avoid use of wing movement by flight in wind speeds. With 40 mph at 55' and 20 mph at sea level the above flight is possible. As the bird dives it enters layers of air moving ever slowly and the air speed of the bird builds more rapidly. With the upward swoop the bird turns into the wind, and thus enters faster moving layers of air – to increase its rising speed.
wave winds.
provide uplift.
Note: Antarctic convergence. 'cold water from the south, meeting warmer Atlantic and Pacific surface water.
line of convergence.
Antarctica.
10.3.03
11.3.03
25.

+ **Silent Sea (No 1-8),** *2003,* Photomontage and paint, 23" x 7"

+ **Arriving Signy,** *South Orkney Islands,* Video of *RRS James Clark Ross* cutting through ice

+ **Sky Blu – Christmas Eve,** *Southern Palmer Land, Antarctic Peninsula,* Large format print (3 x 1.5m), made using the mapping plotter at British Antarctic Survey, Cambridge

+ **Fossil Bluff,** *Palmer Land, Antarctic Peninsula,* Large format print (1.5 x 2m) made using the mapping plotter at British Antarctic Survey, Cambridge

DAVID WHEELER *(2007–2008)*

Antarctica is an extraordinary place to explore the imagination. The extreme environment and physical conditions, combined with the psychological effect of spending time in the remote desert landscape, make it an inspiring and mythical place to work.

Standing on the Antarctic ice-cap, there is a tangible sense of the natural forces and phenomena surrounding us. The experience has led to an ongoing series of performance and music-based work that takes this as a core theme.

+ **Trace,** Video projection and mixed materials

1

2

3

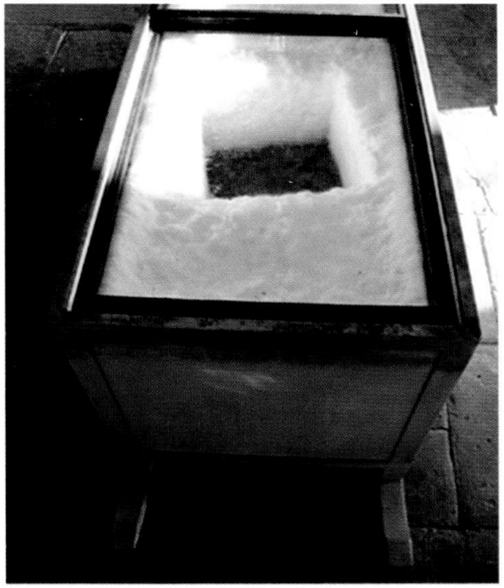

4

5

6

1 **Visible Light – Nightfall,** Steel, industrial freezers, video screen, frost, snow and earth
2 **Visible Light,** Detail
3 **Nightfall,** Detail

4 **Vessel 1 and 2,** Steel, water, compressed air and electronic controller
5 **Slack Water,** Adapted cement mixer, polythene, water and pebbles
6 **Slack Water,** Detail

+ **Travelogue,** *24.10.2007–05.01.2008,* Photographs from Port Stanley to Sky Blu

+ **Electric Field,** *2009,* A site-specific live performance, devised with the IOU project team, for the company's base in Halifax, photographs Porl Medlock

Audio CD
Antarctic Sounds

1. Circumnavigation of Iceberg — 67° 34′ 0″ S, 58° 8′ 0″ W
   (Rothera Bay)
2. Moraine Smelt Water, Uranus Glacier — 71° 20′ 0″ S, 68° 17′ 0″ W
   (Fossil Bluff)
3. Katabatic Wind — 74° 51′ 0″ S, 71° 34′ 0″ W
   (Sky Blu)
4. Adélie Penguin Colony — 60° 30′ 0″ S, 62° 20′ 0″ W
   (Gourlay Point, Signy Island)
5. *RRS James Clark Ross* Encountering the Ice Belt — 64° 30′ 0″ S, 62° 20′ 0″ W
   (Hold Number 2; Gerlache Strait)

Excerpt from
The Guardian Diaries

First published in *Guardian Unlimited*, 2003

The aim was to capture the monumental explosions of the Sheldon Glacier moving slowly into the sea. This thing produces bangs the size of 40 cannons going off at the same time. However, before we could get there we had to traverse Stork Mountain for a couple of miles, covered in snow and ice. Once on the peak, the view of the glacier, the surrounding mountains and the bay was mammoth. We set up Fluffy to record the whole vista in such light winds that it was possible to pick up icebergs crunching miles away in the bay. (Fluffy is the name of my Sennheiser mic. system, which is covered in wind baffling. She has become a bit of a polar legend and everyone down South seems to know her).

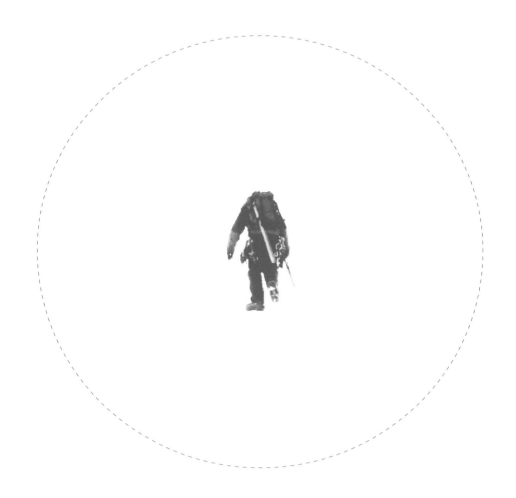

+ For CD, see inside back cover

Blue Whale

from the collection, *Galatea* (Salt: 2006)

In the dark of the museum's unhallowed arcs,
They have hitched high the lazuli coma of her fin,
Lashing the bearded pannier of her craw.
Mortified, bellying the air – Ocean Boudicca –
Gliding as a jumbo jet, the ocean her night-terror.

The philosophic smile brooks all agonies, willing sacrifice,
And the afterthought eye, like a portrait's intimate study,
Plays shadows from the mind's den –
For an apocalypse of all that is undergone,
Unctiously, earnestly, flesh the decoy.

Her gargantuan heart is the holy ark, a fleshy jeroboam
Whose brew is the *weltliebe* wherein the infinite
Possibilities of human love find glittering passage;
Or a subsidiary brain in whose glistening sanctum
Man's *sturm und drang* silts like tealeaves in porcelain.

Subdued to so much meat, she's heavy
In the air, drowning beneath her fathoms,
The mighty eloquence of her breaststroke, attuned
To the echoes of waves, leadens to extinction,
Blood's alchemy conjuring the glorious jeroboam into a tomb.

Everyman has recurring dreams in which he swims
The briars of her veins, intending to the profoundest depths
Of which he might be capable, sifting for perfection
As her magnitude commands. In the dark, all eyes askance,
The memories of her monolithic ego begin to heave.

Excerpt from
***On Extinction:* How we became estranged from nature**

First published in *Granta*, 2011

The British Antarctic Survey's ship, *RRS James Clark Ross,* was anchored in Stanley. I joined the ship in late October for its preliminary crossing of the Southern Ocean to Antarctica. As I walked across the floating platform to its gangplank, I noticed workers unpacking recent shipments of goods in the shadows of an adjacent hold. I darted over to them and was amused to find huge cellophane cubes packed with cans of cola labelled 'Coca Cola Polar'. A terracotta-coloured shipping container housed several hundred orange kitbags, each tagged with the Union Jack and our names. I found mine among them and carried it on to the ship, remembering a summer day in the gear store of the BAS headquarters, trying on fleece underwear and thick, windproof jackets. I took the top bunk in a cabin shared with two other women. The yellow curtains that gave me a little privacy were William Morris-like designs of exoticised woodland weeds. Once we were at sea, they began to inspire odd, contorted dreams of home.

In recent years, a number of scientists involved with the BAS had received international praise for their research into the importance of the Southern Ocean for global climate, analysing 18 of 24 climate models for the assessment report of the Intergovernmental Panel on Climate Change published in 2007. Much of the science explored dynamic processes that characterise transition zones such as oceanic fronts – areas where two bodies of water with considerably different characteristics meet – or the jagged boundary between the sea ice and open water that fringes the Antarctic continent. One well-known boundary is the Polar Front. Along its edges, warmer, subantarctic waters touch the cold polar waters of Antarctica. Superstition and a sudden chill mark the crossing of its mist-blurred line, the water temperature plummeting by around four degrees. We made our crossing of this boundary on 29 October 2007, a fluid feature that many scientists regard to be the movable threshold of Antarctica. The following day the American Senate debated the possible ratification of the 'Laws of the Sea', described as "possibly the most significant legal instrument of this century" by the United Nations Secretary General in 1982. Those nations signed up to it were party to common rules on navigation, fishing and the economic development of the open seas. The pursuit of deep-sea mining interests had kept American governments from adopting the treaty in the past and they failed to endorse it on this occasion too.

Shortly after crossing the Polar Front, I witnessed my first iceberg, its colossal separation from air and ocean, its lunar defiance, intractable against the elements. One façade was rough and quite white but as we swung forwards I saw its slope of aquamarine, smooth as a cheek.

We arrived at South Georgia in early November. The small number of buildings that lined the shore housed one of the British Antarctic Survey research bases and the government of these remote, ice-struck islands. One of the first individuals in the world to sight them was London merchant Antoine de la Roché, when strong winds blew his ship off course in 1675. But James Cook, a sea captain from Whitby in Yorkshire, became the first to land on the islands of his own volition when his ship, the *Resolution*, anchored in January 1775, flagging the islands as British. Shortly afterwards, they were named after King George III.

Within a decade of Cook's account of the large number of fur and elephant seals encountered there, sealers from Britain and North America began visiting South Georgia, shipping thousands of seal skins to home markets and trading skins and oils with China.

I hauled on a pair of snow boots, some padded salopettes, and a bright orange BAS jacket, and clambered from the *James Clark Ross* on to the jetty at King Edward Point harbour. The ship loomed large, its shadow casting a giant trapezium across the snow. The name belonged in the past to a vessel of a quite different character, a Norwegian whaling factory ship that hunted from the waters beyond these shores. On Christmas Eve, 1923, the Norwegian *James Clark Ross*, under the command of Captain Carl Larsen, was hunting for blue whales in the Ross Sea. Over 200 whales were slaughtered that season, yielding 17,000 barrels of oil. This was the first time the whalers succeeded in flensing their entire catch alongside the ship, enabling them to stay at sea. Until then, whalers nearly always returned to shore to process their catch. All of the commercial whaling countries experimented with different methods to escape this inconvenience. Sometimes a wooden cutting platform was lowered on to the whale's carcass, on which the whalers balanced precariously, slicing rings of blubber as if carefully peeling an apple.

A year later, engineers succeeded in fitting rear slipways of staggering length on to the factory ship the *Lancer*, enabling the vessel to process whales entirely at sea. In less than 10 years, the blue whales captured were noticeably smaller than those taken in previous decades, suggesting that nearly half the catch was sexually immature and that the population was in danger of disappearance. The large baleen whales reached sexual maturity at a leisurely pace, their pregnancies lasting for around a year. The population wasn't adapted to replace itself under such threats.

Across the sound from King Edward Point was Grytviken, the ruins of the earliest shore whaling station in the Southern Ocean, established by Captain Larsen. Grytviken, or 'pot cove', was so named by the Swedish Antarctic Expedition in 1902 after the large number of cast iron pots left on the beach, once used to boil up elephant-seal blubber. I made my way towards the ruins, accompanied by a couple of scientists and the ship's doctor. It was a dizzying morning. Sunlight embroidered every surface, such that I had to squint to see the snow-covered path ahead. Before leaving, one of the field assistants had urged me to wear sunglasses. In weather like this, he told me, the snow could blind a person not wearing sunglasses in a few hours, erasing all senses to its defiant blankness. I lumbered prudently along the snow-lipped edges of the brash ice, whose startled white waves hid the immense fullness of the elephant seals. In the distance, I could see a complex of giant rusted structures against the snow. Beyond these ruins was the spire of a white and red church and the source of a stream that wound down to the shoreline, where an old whaler and harpoon were stuck in the sludge. The belching and huffing din of the seals lessened and, at first, all was quiet. Then I took a few steps further and everywhere there was the sound of dripping water, oddly sanctifying cadences against a backdrop of furnace and factory.

The first thing that I encountered was a wooden building that housed a small museum. Steps led up to its olive-green entrance, where a cream plaque read 'OPEN'. Inside, I slowly meandered through its narration of Grytviken's whaling past. The previous evening I had read the diaries of Willem Van der Does, who worked aboard the first *James Clark Ross*. His memories resonated in my mind, images of the ship dragging seven whale cadavers through the thronging snow squalls. Under the fazing tilt of the waves, the blubber and meat cutters crawled over the mouldering bulks, propping themselves on the carcasses, hacking and slicing. They carved off the whales' lips to reach the baleen, and chopped the great tongue away with an axe. They found rudiments of rear limbs invisible from the outside. "The whales are creatures that are doomed to disappear from the earth," remarked Van der Does in 1934, "despite all legal measures to prevent it."

Humans have occasionally captured or made use of stranded whales since prehistoric times. The first organised whale fishery was in the Bay of Biscay, established by Basque hunters in the Middle Ages. These whalers pursued the slower baleen whales, bowhead and grey whales, flinging harpoons at them multiple times in order to kill them. After exhausting whale populations in northern latitudes during the seventeenth and eighteenth centuries, European and North American whalers expanded southwards, innovating new technologies to do so. One nineteenth-century company listed the needs of the whaling ships in arresting detail: food, from flour, vinegar, preserved meats and cheeses to souchong tea and chocolate. A complete set of crockery. A complete set of tinware, from pans to a ladle and oil skimmer. A tin-coated blubber-room lamp and cook's lantern. A huge range of tools for making ship repairs, anvils, axes, adzes, jack planes, and general hardware, from coffee mills to handcuffs. And, of course, the specialised tools: blubber forks, blubber mincing knives, rigging leather, friction rollers, pikes, toggles, harpoons, and fluke chain rings.

The traditional whaling society of Norway pioneered many of the new devices that allowed the whale hunt to begin in the Southern Ocean around South Georgia. First came faster whaling vessels powered by steam, then the explosive grenade-harpoon, the shore stations, and finally the floating factory ships. At the heart of the onshore stations was the flensing platform, on which the dead bodies of the whales were winched for butchering. Blubber was sliced away and boiled up in tripots to produce oil. The skeletons of the beasts were mechanically hoisted into huge bone lofts then rendered into more oil. Oil was stored in gigantic metal tanks, and any remaining parts of the beasts were rendered down for bone meal. Initially, the whalers dumped the bones and the unwanted meat in the bay in front of the station but soon the British enacted laws requiring full utilisation of the carcass. This was the absolute industrialisation of the hunting of the whale, and the mechanised mass appropriation to human needs of a complex living creature formed over millions of years.

After leaving the museum, I wandered around the ruins, trying to guess the purpose of each rusty structure. I struggled to imagine what it must have been like when still active, the smell of butchered and burning meat, the clinking sounds of winched carcasses, the daily chatter of the workers. A young British whaler called Davies encountered the *James Clark Ross* at sea near South Georgia in 1949. In his diary, he described the ship's siren rising higher and higher until it made the sailors' heads ache and their ears sing. This noise, he said, mingled with the dense fog to give the whole scene an eerie quality. The sights were so surreal that the trip seemed "all a long dream" to him. Davies commented that it didn't take long for the realities of whaling to stamp out any sense of romance and adventure. Once this disenchantment hit the whalers, he admitted, they saw only a marine slaughterhouse, with uncertain prospects of a good bonus for such tough and bloody work.

I crept through the iron shadows of a large building, its corrugated walls stripped to the sturdy bones of its construction. Water dripped from its metal joists, an uncanny timekeeper. In one of the far rooms, there was the vague, blanched outline of a human head and shoulders chalked into the rust.

Beyond this large building, freakish instruments and workings cluttered the landscape. There was an overgrown toothed object like a saw, curved and as beautiful as a Norse carving. I could see chains under fragile bonnets of snow with links bigger than my hands. In the distance, the disintegrating platforms of mortuary metal were apparent, proportioned to the massive bodies of whales. A short walk away from the strandline, I stumbled across a large tarnished tank on which the words 'BLUBBER COOKERY' were painted in faded white lettering. At the front was a bolted, square-shaped opening. I immediately thought of the pictures in my childhood copy of *Hansel and Gretel*, the entrance into the oven where the siblings shoved the witch who held them captive to satisfy her monstrous appetite. But perhaps most startling of all was one of several oil vats, a round structure of astounding proportions, bulging through time and disuse. Sunlight nudged into its snowy circular border, and I too nudged forward, amazed, appalled, snow falling soundlessly around me.

Also from
On Extinction

As we neared Bird Island, half a mile off the mainland of South Georgia, the winds grew stronger and the sky became a scaffold of clouds in greys of iron and steel. The *James Clark Ross* sought shelter in the bay at Elsehul, where the crew dropped anchor, and the ship heeled and pitched on the waves. In the distance, we could see the raked outline of Bird Island, only its highest reaches soothed by snow. James Cook sighted the island on his second voyage in search of the fabled southern continent in 1775. Cook didn't think much of the tiny island or of South Georgia in its entirety. "Wild rocks raised their lofty summits," he commented, "til they were lost in the clouds, and the valleys lay covered with everlasting snow." Before the sun went down, I stood out on the deck watching black-browed and light-mantled sooty albatrosses carving the air, sweeping upwards, lassoing the sky; and white-chinned petrels as black as the night, harbingers of the oncoming darkness. There had been a silvery edginess to the day, as if the world was unnerved by the gathering weather. The ocean was an ominous, gunmetal grey, and a single wandering albatross drifted alongside the ship, its wings tipped to the sea as if to overhear the waves.

The following morning, the weather was clement enough to allow us to take the smaller boats ashore. A massive, contorted, bright blue iceberg challenged the entrance to the bay, and penguins and seals nudged up the waves, then quickly slapped down under the water. Ahead of us, the beach was jostling with aggressive young male fur seals. Landing at a small wooden platform, we formed a nervous line, edging past the snarling and huffing mature bull seals towards the little research base at the head of the beach. The sealers who passed the island in the interwar years observed no more than a handful of fur seals, which were, by then, nearly extinct through hunting. Isolation and protection has since enabled their revival to such an extent that the precious stumps of tussock grass rising from the shoreline of the island are being eroded as the creatures push beyond the bounds of their overcrowded littoral territories.

Bird Island was the wildest landscape I had ever experienced. The prolific stench of animal life, dead and living, made me giddy. As I hiked up a frozen stream, the racket of survival on the beach below gradually faded to nothing. A pair of black wings, like those of a fallen angel, lay in the middle of the snow-covered stream, its hinges of gristle still intact. As I ascended the hill, I seemed to stride back through eons to the primeval past. On giant clumps of dead and living tussock grass were the wondrous aboriginals of the young wandering albatrosses. I stared in amazement at the old beardedness of their white plumage, the snare of their long, hooked beaks, the perceptiveness of their round, pitch-black eyes. Although the ancestors of these birds probably began to twist into shape over 50 million years ago, the first confirmed albatross fossils date from the Oligocene epoch, around 30 million years later. Between the Eocene and the Oligocene, the extinction of large numbers of plants and animals took place, especially marine creatures like archaeocetes, ancient whales. But the diversity of life gradually recovered through the many millennia of the Oligocene and new forms appeared, some of which eventually evolved into the whales and albatrosses alive today.

During this time, the land masses of Antarctica and Australia slowly wrenched apart, altering the world's oceans. The isolating flow of the great Antarctic Circumpolar Current swirled into force around 30 million years ago, establishing the polar fronts and the icy quarantine of the great, heart-shaped southern continent. Ever since, the size and extent of the Antarctic and Arctic ice caps have changed the traits of the oceans, bringing about adaptations both physical and territorial to seabirds like albatrosses. I found it a curiously exciting thought that albatrosses once took flight from shores closer to home. In the final decade of the nineteenth century, the British geologist Richard Lydekker scraped some bones from Suffolk crags around two million years old that he named *Diomedea anglica,* the English albatross, an extinct bird somewhere between the short-tailed and great albatross species. The bones were evidence that some species of albatross once bred in the North Atlantic, but that the transformations of the Earth forced them to retreat steadily southward. Just imagining this prior reality set the compass of my mind spinning.

Bird Island was a trackless and tempestuous landscape, a wild land where natural forces reigned. As I stood on the mull of the hill, the fragile fortifications of the icebergs holding their line against the stormy seas below, my mind turned even further back, to riotous landscapes of prehistoric forests, jungled and unbroken, to times when nature alone transfigured Earth, not the technologies of humanity. Over 400 million years ago, the early clutch of exotic plants began their lustrous capture of the landscape. The first, monstrous forests emerged from giant horsetails, ferns taller than several men standing on one another's shoulders, and the simple, olive-green club mosses. After this, grew the beautiful cycads and conifers, their nuts and kernels trumpeting their fertility, and giant ferns that sheltered little revolutionary blisters of pollen. These presaged the flowering beauty of our world, such as the exquisite, magnolia-like *Archaeanthus linnenbergeri,* 98 million years old, with its six generous curls of petals and the dissected hearts of its leaves. And the buzz and dart of insects and birds, their lives strung on the scents and dusts and fruits of these early flowers. No such wildernesses as these exist anywhere in the world today, not even on Bird Island. Our influence is too pervasive. But Earth's astounding potential is there, recorded with almost photographic precision in its rocks, soils and ice. From these, we know of times and landscapes absolutely outlandish to our imaginings.

Postcards From South Georgia

Originally broadcast on 'The Verb', Radio 3, September 2007

The first iceberg was seen yesterday, late in the evening, lit from within by a cold blue light. In the distance, the dark shadow of a whale's tail lifted briefly from the water.

This morning, I go out onto the top deck at six in the morning, ready for what everyone tells me will be a breathtaking first sight of South Georgia, but there is only mist and drizzle and a calm grey sea. It's too cold to wait outside, so I go back to my cabin, check my email, and discover that it's snowing at home. When I get back to the top deck, the three marine biologists and a boatman for whom this small corner of South Georgia will soon be home are standing up against the railing, speechless with awe.

The day before, I'd asked them how they felt about being away from home for such a long contract. Two years seems like a long time I said, with no holidays. They told me it wasn't that long at all, not really, that they were still young, that the experience was going to more than make up for the difficulties of being away from home, and they said these things with a practised tone, as if it wasn't the first time they'd had to answer the question. This morning, I can understand their lack of hesitation.

The mist has burnt away in the morning sun, lifting the curtain on a shifting pack of icebergs, great blocks and twists and spires of ice in grey and blue and white, which slide apart to reveal the tiny wooden buildings of the research base, dwarfed by the mountainous grandeur of the bay. "I just can't believe we're going to live here", one of the biologists says, and there's not a shadow of trepidation in his voice. The last of the mist hangs in folds along the snowline of the mountain ridges, the sky a deep rich blue behind it. Below, albatrosses and petrels and terns circle above grassy slopes and fast-flowing streams. At the water's edge, the sandy-grey boulders turn out to be elephant seals basking in the sun, and fur seals, and, as we move closer, king penguins.

At the end of the bay, rusting into the ground, is the abandoned whaling station of Grytviken. Around 80 per cent of the world's whales were caught from this station and from the few nearby, and for the first 20 years of operations, the harpoon ships barely needed to leave the bay for their kills. Fish in barrels have had higher survival rates.

In a museum, housed in the old manager's villa, photographs show the whalers playing football, reading on their bunks, waving at the camera as they clamber through the flensed carcasses of their catch. Some of them are buried on the hillside, next to Ernest Shackleton, the explorer. Their houses and workshops are collapsing now, the cinema long gone, the whalebones crumbling slowly into dust along the shore. The skeletal wrecks of their ships are still tied up against the jetty, sinking, overlooked by the museum and its neatly painted collection of industrial remnants – harpoon guns, bone-saws, blubber-spades. There's a logbook inside the museum for visitors to record whale sightings, however brief or uncertain they might be, and if it's an attempt to reassure us that we stopped in time, then it feels like a futile one.

In the newly restored church, a Norwegian clapboard building with a bell tower and steps leading up to the porch, I meet a wind-tanned man with a North American accent and a baseball cap, sitting on one of the heavy wooden pews. He came in on a yacht, he tells me, he's down here for a holiday and it's not the first time either. He's wearing a neatly trimmed white beard and the weather-worn clothes of someone used to being outdoors, a knife strapped to his belt. "Came all the way from northern Alaska", he announces, proudly. "I like it down here", he adds, glancing at the ice-streaked mountains just outside the window. "Kind of reminds me of home, I guess".

I think of the Arctic tern, one of the world's smallest seabirds which makes an annual migration from the northern to the southern polar circles; a perilous and exhausting journey which decimates their numbers. And when they finally arrive they find a landscape which kind of reminds them of home.

I walk round the bay, taking wide detours past the territorial seals and their pups, walking past the small cemetery and up onto the headland. Across the still clear water I can see the bright red ship which has been my home for two weeks, and will be my home for another four, her decks and cranes dwarfing the huts of the research base. She'll be leaving dock in a few hours time, and I'll be confined again to that shrunken airless world of cabin and laboratory and bar. I stride out across the wet tussock grass, hauling reserves of fresh air into my lungs.

Around a ridge, almost hidden in a low boggy hollow, I come across the crumpled remains of a helicopter sinking into the ground, scoured by the weather to a gleaming stainless steel. This, along with a few scattered shell casings along the clifftops, is all that's left from the brief conflict in 1982, when the Falklands War lurched southwards to tussle over these quiet unpopulated rocks. It was a playground-sized battle, over in a couple of days, but it still left a dozen Argentinian boys buried in the cemetery with the whalers and Shackleton. I squelch towards the helicopter to take a closer look, but am beaten back by the swooping attacks of a tern, anxious to protect its nest.

In the evening, before dinner and far, far too soon, we leave Grytviken behind. Two container loads of supplies have been delivered, and a year's worth of waste collected. Our passports have all been stamped by the postmistress, and the four new members of staff put into place. They stand on the jetty edge, with their new colleagues and companions, surrounded by vast mountains and sea and ice and sky, the sound of calving glaciers echoing across the bay. They look very small as the ship slips away from her moorings, squinting up at us, craning their necks, waving.

We head further south, towards the ice.

Extract from
The Forgotten Man Of The Antarctic

First published in *Guardian Weekend* magazine, June 2007

On a good day, the sub-Antarctic island of South Georgia can be astoundingly beautiful. Mountains rear up from the shoreline and across the island's spine, crammed in, one upon the other, sheer faces of ice and snow glistening in the pure clear air. Melt water falls from cliffs of tussock and moss, tumbling through tarns and streams to the sea. Elephant seals wallow on the sheltered beaches, albatrosses and terns circle overhead, penguins gather and wait and watch. Icebergs drift and bump in the bay, breaking apart with low explosive booms which tremble across the otherwise glass-still sea.

South Georgia has very few good days.

On a bad day, South Georgia is wet and grey and ferociously cold. Driving winds and blizzards are not unusual, visibility is often poor, and conditions are such that anyone living and working there can reckon on spending two-thirds of their time indoors, waiting for the weather to improve; anyone foolish enough not to wait would be putting themselves at great risk of exposure, hypothermia, and death. It's a brutal, unforgiving and desperately isolated place. Which is, of course, part of the attraction.

May 20, 1961 was a particularly bad day in South Georgia. When Duncan Carse – explorer, radio actor, and now experimenter in solitude – woke up in the early hours of the morning he could already hear waves breaking against the walls of his small wooden hut. This was strange, because he'd sited it on relatively high ground in one of the most sheltered harbours on the southern coast of the island, and had never even heard waves in the cove before. He heard the roar of shingle being thrown against the walls, and sat up, and with the next breaking wave the cabin was smashed around him, the sea pouring up and over him and pinning him to his bed until he was convinced he would drown.

This wasn't part of the plan.

When the waters finally subsided, he scrambled under the fallen walls of the cabin and up onto higher ground before another wave broke over the beach, standing in his long-johns and vest in the cold wet light of early morning with the cove under water and his possessions being washed out to sea. It took him a few minutes to move beyond the shock and fear and do something about his immediate situation – a few minutes in which, wet and half-naked, his body had already moved into the first stages of hypothermia. Rushing back to the cabin, he found two sealed kitbags in what remained of the hut's doorway, and two odd boots, and managed to dress himself in dry clothes before the next wave swept up the beach.

Over the next few hours, he was able to recover enough equipment and supplies from the wreckage scattered along the shore to ensure his immediate survival. As well as the clothes, he found a tent, sleeping bags, a cooking stove and pans, matches, and tobacco. He found a case of burgundy he'd been saving for a special occasion, and immediately opened the first of many bottles. He found food, and fuel, and his box of books and papers. Much was lost; meteorological equipment, medical supplies, his gramophone player and Harry Belafonte records, a pair of stuffed toys, a set of carpenter's tools. But by the end of the day, drunk and hysterical and soaked by several falls into the waves which continued to surge high up the beach, he'd somehow managed to establish a new camp, sealing himself into his sleeping bag as darkness fell.

He stayed in his tent for three days, drinking heavily, not eating, drifting in and out of consciousness, and when he finally sobered up he wrote this single despairing line in his diary; "I am afraid, and my heart is broken."

This definitely wasn't part of the plan.

*

And it had been such a simple plan. He would go to Undine South Harbour, a sheltered cove on the unpopulated southern coast of South Georgia, build a wooden hut, and live there in absolute solitude for at least 18 months. He would prove that a life lived alone could be rewarding and fruitful – he planned a comprehensive programme of scientific research while he was there – and then return home, when he was ready, to the welcome of a hero. Duncan Carse, the forgotten man of Antarctic exploration, would have triumphed at last.

"I am disillusioned with my fellow men," he announced at a press conference before he left. "Since I was a boy, I have yearned to live an existence away from it all, and with middle age the feeling is irresistible. I am not running away from anything. I hope to find something. I think I will become a stronger character."

He'd been there for three months when the wave struck. It had taken him most of that time to unpack the 10 tons of supplies he'd had shipped out, and to build the wooden hut, and he'd been prevented from starting work on his research programme by a serious leg injury which had confined him to his bunk for a fortnight. Even before the events of that day, the project had begun badly, and his over-riding thought, as he lay in that small tent listening to the storm washing away the last of his possessions, was one which had haunted him throughout his life. He'd failed again.

Writing on Antarctica

The challenge of writing about Antarctica, and especially of writing fiction about Antarctica, is an amplified version of the central challenge of writing itself: how to use language to communicate that which isn't itself word-bound. With most writing, it's possible to draw on the assumption of some level of shared experience: I can trust that the reader will know what I mean by 'tree', for example, or 'car', or 'cloud'. I may wish to add that the tree was tall, or gnarled, or bleached bone-white in the frosted light of the sun; but I don't need to explain what a tree is. This assumption of shared experience is how language itself operates, of course, but it's also something which descriptive writing is able to draw upon. But when it comes to writing about Antarctica, the central problem is that the experience of having been there cannot be assumed to be a shared one. Still, after a century of exploration, and a couple of decades of organised tourism, those who have been to the southern continent are in a very small minority. So the writer is unable to assume an understanding of ice floes, or crevasses, or extremes of dry cold, or the peculiar tricks of perspective which result from a landscape without feature seen through incredibly clean air. And the writer is also unable to assume a familiarity with the strange combinations of claustrophobia and isolation which come from living in very small co-dependent communities a very long way from home; nor of the experience of 24-hour daylight; nor of the effect of vast emptiness on the psyche. And without access to the shorthand of shared experience, the writer will always struggle to push the writing beyond something which is simply 'about' Antarctica into being something which comes from Antarctica.

Put simply, it's really, *really* hard to describe an iceberg.

The work which has so far emerged from my experience as a writer-in-residence with the British Antarctic Survey in 2004 has all been non-fiction. Partly this is because there are so many great stories which have still not been fully told; but partly it's because I'm still, years later, struggling to find a fictional form which is able to overcome this problem of unshared experiences. I'm still working at it though: my drafts and sketches to date seem to be building on the idea that the 'Great Antarctic Novel' probably won't feature icebergs at all, that what is interesting about the Antarctic experience lies in the relationship between *There* and *Home*, in the heroic self-image, in the play between absence and presence, in the yearning for a solitude which depends on other people, in the classic Antarctic themes of disappointment and failure.

It seems likely that the setting for the 'Great Antarctic Novel' will be closer to a suburban garden in Cambridgeshire than the exposed headlands of Rothera. It seems almost inevitable that a shed – emblematic of the male self-image and drive to solitude and self-sufficiency which lie behind much Antarctic mythology – will play a central role. I'm getting there, slowly. And as Cherry-Garrard probably kept saying to himself on that terrible and ultimately rather pointless journey to fetch the penguin's egg: I'll get there, in the end.

The two extracts included here are from an article on Duncan Carse which I wrote for *Guardian Weekend* magazine, on his failed 'Experiment At Living Alone On The Coast Of South Georgia'; and from a series of 100-word postcards which I emailed home during my time in Antarctica.

I remain deeply grateful to the British Antarctic Survey and Arts Council England for the opportunity to take part in the Artists & Writers programme, and look forward to rewarding their patience in due course...

Extract from
The Ice Lovers

First published by McArthur & Company, Toronto, 2009

It is winter now. All around the continent the ice tightens its grip. Beneath the surface, winter water is collecting in thermodynamic columns of vertical mixing; threaded through them is a deep layer of very cold surface water. As water cools, it gels on the surface. Hydrostatic pressures are higher on the floating ice shelves, and this lowers the freezing temperature of the water, and the ocean below the ice shelf deepens its frost. Deep in the ocean, far beneath the continent, Antarctic bottom water churns, dense, depthless, blind with blackness. The Antarctic icefield is a self-reinforcing system: land, water, air – they all depend on the ice. Ice makes more of itself, becomes more itself. In becoming, its being is strengthened. The pack forms.

Water is slow: the Antarctic circumpolar waters circulate the world oceans every thousand years, creating velocities of cold, eddies, thermal columns which govern the great currents of the oceans – the Gulf Stream, the Humboldt – which affect the planet's climate. In this process, the sea ice is key; it acquires structure through sinews of ice crystals, it melds, binds into a static ice sculpture garden. Less is known about the continent, its processes, its intents, than anywhere else in the world, apart from the deep oceans. It is a cold terrestrial moon, another planet, this cold node of the known world.

The day of the plane's departure was overcast and cold. Nara walked over to the plane alone along the gravel path leading past the accommodation block and across the runway. She found Luke in the hangar, supervising the payload, calculating fuel. She watched as they loaded the plane. She said goodbye to the summer base commander, to the Met man, who had left his five-day forecast behind for the winterers, pinned to the flight map. After that they would have to predict the weather for themselves. Luke emerged from the fuselage.

He was wearing his orange Ventile jacket, the one he had worn in their days in the Ellsworths. He had told her how this jacket had been invented during the Second World War, how it had saved the lives of Allied pilots who crashed in Greenland, in Iceland.

"That's its genius: the wind passes through you, but you don't feel it."

Now he said, "I almost want to say, if you need anything, let me know."

"I know, but you can't help me, here."

"No, I can't."

The chief pilot was calling him from within. Luke turned to her. His expression was difficult to read: ecstatic, but grave; a grain of regret, but also the happiness of release.

He said, "I'll see you in October."

She nearly said goodbye, but at the last minute caught herself.

The door is closed with a groan more human than mechanical, and the plane's propellers start to chop at the air slowly at first, in fits and starts, then building to a smooth rotation. The plane remains on the apron, all four propellers spinning, the plane trembling while the pilots run through their checklist and speak to Stanley on the HF for the latest weather. Then the plane begins to move, tentatively at first, as if it has not yet decided to leave. It taxis to the southern edge of the runway where it executes a deft, balletic turn, and lines up at the end of the airstrip, where it stands, its trembling now a shudder. A roar, and gravel spews as it charges. It is already flying when it passes the hangar apron. When the plane has cleared the icebergs in the cove it climbs sharp, then banks right to turn around the peninsula where it disappears, hidden by the hill back of base. When it reappears, it is flying low for the traditional fly-by past the comms tower. At the height of the laboratory roof it comes back over the runway, the propellers whipping the dust. Behind her the cook says, "holy fuck".

Just at the moment when the plane's position seems untenable, when gravity is about to reach up to snatch it, the pilots climb and the plane soars over their heads. She sees the pale underbelly of the fuselage, hears the roar of the propellers as they chew the air above her. A single shaft of silver sun breaks through the clouds and flashes off the fuselage. The silver slash stays with it as the plane journeys upward and begins to be consumed by cloud. She watches as these points of silver light congeal in her mind, absorbing their negative radiance, the grey of clouds, lead and pewter dispersing, until she is only looking at a place in the sky where the plane had been.

The Antarctic Convergence

A sequence of short poems from
Night Orders: Poems from Antarctica and the Arctic

First published by Smith/Doorstop books and the Environment Institute, University College London, 2011

Uncharted Waters

Sleeking through
dead men names: Brabant, Livingston, Biscoe
the Graham Coast. Sixteen knots
in uncharted waters.
To the west, the Bellingshausen
Abyssal plain, the Charcot
Deep-Sea Fan.
Names here are less lunar
than places you might
fight an unwinnable war: the Sentinel Range
The Heritage Mountains.
Names borrowed
from the expired rapture
of long-departed boots:
Doake Ice Rumples, Dufek Massif
Two favourites: Whichhaway Nunataks
The Executive Committee Range.
Soon we will stand
where no others have. I never hoped
to be the first at anything, or anywhere
All night we will pick our way
between reefs and islets
on radar, charts, instinct. Tonight
the Master will not sleep.

Magnetic Poles

A wandering magnetism.
The spike and guile of him.
The south magnetic pole is where the Earth's
magnetic fields are vertically aligned.
The pole can move very rapidly,
sometimes hundreds of kilometres a day.
Sometimes it's not in the Antarctic at all
but a hundred kilometres
out in the ocean.
He tells me the planet's alignment is changing
energy fields will be turned inside out.
The last time this happened on Earth
humans didn't exist. Whales and birds
and eels will lose their bearings, their
migrations stalling.
We will all be southerners then.

The Ordinary Year

Sidereal time, ephemeris time, mean solar days, Zulu Time. I learn that the sidereal year is the time it takes the Earth to make one complete orbit of the sun – 365.25636 days, a little longer than the ordinary solar year. Its official name is that: the Ordinary Year. No ordinary year, this. Suddenly I am on a loop. A winter childhood: snow, trailers, formica. Trailing behind other peoples' existences. Linoleum on the walls, shotguns in the bedroom, cars that won't start. Coming at the base from the back end of the Point – radio transmitters emitting radiation, gigantic Julian the man-mountain driving around in a Gator. Piles of rubble, drums, boxes, corrugated iron arch sheds, all strung between tower lines like a cross between a granite quarry and a penal colony. But then you walk around the Point and the base disappears and you hear only the groan and rustle of icebergs melting, a wide ring of mountains, and you are in the Antarctic. Then back to the penal colony after a trip to the Monument, a reminder that people died here, that it is a dangerous place.

Salinometer

All night we take measurements
from a device that looks like
an ice cream machine.
He funnels the bottles, I record the numbers.
We are beneath the waterline
technically submerged.
He tells me Seism means shock.
that an elastic medium
can be subjected to two types of deformation:
compression and shear.
The language of ice
is one of rent and quiver.
I tell him about other kinds
of stress and flux: *Ludus, Storge, Mania,*
Pragma, Eros. He tells me
P waves and S waves are determined
by elastic parameters.
Ice scrapes against the hull.
If we put our hands
on the walls we can feel the ridges
as we grind through.
All night we feel the ice this way
sometimes emerging onto the deck
for air and see the *chien-loup* –
what cinematographers call twilight:
the wolfhound.
The mountains are wolfish too
winter cousins in storm cloaks.
We glide through
a rose-grey perpetual dusk.
Our shift ends at breakfast
we climb up above deck
for coffee.

The Tagging Board

These are the places we can be:
On Base, Flying, Off Base,
Runway, Bonner Lab
Vals, Boat House
Around the Point

the field assistant
nearly died 300 metres from our front door
slipped down an ice cliff
slid onto an ice shelf
could have tried to swim
but you won't last five minutes in this water
he forgot to tag out
so he wasn't found until morning
(alive)

clever staircases
of salvation
winding up and down.

Thresholds

They talk about hope here about
having a durable heart
but ignition is forbidden
because we fear fire.
The creatures in the aquarium
are being probed for the upper
temperature threshold
of their survivability.
They are burning too
but slowly. As Shackleton said
we are reduced to 'the naked soul of man'.
But rather than succumb to despair
we grow and grow
giants of the plateau
our hearts exploding.

Also from
Night Orders: Poems from Antarctica and the Arctic

Endurance

We call the ship that has come to pluck us out
our big red taxi. Its real name is the *Endurance*
a namesake of Shackleton's
broken vessel.
It is April. Leaving Antarctica in winter
is like slouching away from a doomed village:
tidepools now clogged with ice,
a gorged sky. Time passes like saints
watching their backs.
The horizon is a blue strip of light
between ice and sea, cloud and mountain.
We live like liar peasants.
The air only hooks. Struck dumb to find
we are enemies of ourselves
in an obsessive present.
We used to know so many things.
Now we are strung on
one thin rule:
not far now
until the darkness.

Visions Of Antarctica

For many people, the word Antarctic carries with it many pejorative overtones, triggering thoughts of unpitying cold, of isolation and of the death of explorers. Such strong reactions to a place few will ever visit is a testimony to the media's enthusiasm for bringing the continent to public life through articles and documentaries, especially during this centenary period for many of the great journeys of exploration. In considering how the continent has been visually portrayed, there are few people who would think of any medium other than photography and while that has undoubtedly been successful, there are other visions of the landscape and place that interpret its beauty and illuminate its importance in more individual, and perhaps emotional, ways. It may be surprising that these alternative approaches to visions of the Antarctic stretch back over 200 years and in the last 50 years in particular, have become increasingly diverse as poetry and music have joined painting and plays in the search for a broader understanding to complement the deluge of science coming out of the continent. In this essay, I want to look at how and why these non-scientific views first began, and what might be the common links between arts and science in their parallel search for some version of the truth.

Context is often a potent source of explanations and it is in the history of exploration we need to look first for the dawning of Antarctic art. While sailing the world to chart the seas, map the lands and claim new territories for the Crown were the principal drivers for many of the early explorers, for at least some of them the opportunities to conduct scientific observations, collect specimens and data and document new features of the world were at least equally important. In many parts of the world there were other cultures and people to encounter and exploit, other literatures and religions to understand, and unknown resources to develop. But for explorers in the polar areas, things were different. True, in the north there were the Inuit, the Lapps and the many Siberian tribes to contend with, but in the Antarctic there was only the ice and the weather to challenge them. They brought back with them tales of adventure, new maps and a variety of visions of this remote continent.

The early polar explorers had great hopes of finding riches in the icy wastes, credulously swallowing the theories of the cartographers in terms of the likely size of the regions and the extent of lands to be found there. The Ortelius world map of 1570 showed a huge continent around the South Pole, a prize to spur on any explorer. With Captain Cook's voyages in the late eighteenth century we began to see, not only the limits of this continent, but also that this remote land was covered by inhospitable ice, a feature investigated more fully in the early nineteenth century by expeditions led by Charles Wilkes, Jules-Sebastien-Cesar Dumont D'Urville and Thaddeus Bellinghausen, who concluded the area was useless. It was not until the British expedition of 1839–43 led by James Clark Ross that some accurate descriptions of the difficulties in accessing both the coast and the interior were first appreciated. These expeditions have provided us with the earliest Antarctic art, as they all carried artists of some sort to record the new lands and species and it is here that our visions begin. These early pictures and drawings were meant for practical use, to illustrate the coastline or the ice-strewn sea for mariners, to represent the birds and seals for scientists – in short, to create representational images rather than imaginative ones. These requirements became more easily dealt with by photography from the late nineteenth century onwards which meant that interpretive and imaginative art could then begin to flourish, although only pursued by amateurs as there were still considerable difficulties in any professional artists or scholars getting to the continent.

Until very recently, difficulties in accessing the Antarctic have certainly limited the possibilities for writers and artists to experience the continent and use its special magic to stir their imagination. Some of the artistic elements we immediately associate with the continent – like Ralph Vaughan Williams' *Sinfonia Antarctica* and *The Rime of the Ancient Mariner* by Samuel Taylor Coleridge – were pure flights of the imagination as neither had the chance to get anywhere near the poles. Instead, Vaughan Williams used the account of Scott's last expedition as the basis for inspiring his music for the film *Scott of the Antarctic* (1948) and, developing this later into the symphony (1953), he included a quotation from Scott's journal at the start of the fifth movement. Coleridge, on the other hand, was not writing about the Antarctic at all but using the albatross in an allegorical examination of loneliness, guilt and retribution. Yet in choosing his subject, he may have been inspired by Cook's second voyage as his tutor had been William Wales, the astronomer who travelled with Cook!

By the end of the nineteenth century, there were adventurous artists and writers who had taken opportunities offered by individual private expeditions to collect that most important personal experience. While we might immediately think of the professional photographers Frank Hurley and Herbert Ponting on the Mawson, Shackleton and Scott expeditions, there were other artists, but almost exclusively amateur ones, like Edward Wilson with Scott, George Marston with Shackleton, and John Edward Davis with James Clark Ross. In this respect, perhaps William Gordon Burn Murdoch, who went with the Dundee Antarctic Whaling Expedition in 1892, and David Paige, who went with Byrd's Second Antarctic Expedition in 1933–1935, were atypical in being professional artists.

The present preoccupation with science in Antarctica stems quite clearly from the objectives of the International Geophysical Year (IGY) 1957–1958. This extraordinary collaborative venture took place at the height of the Cold War and brought together many countries that were quite antagonistic towards each other. Not only were the Soviet Union and the USA major participants, but the UK, Argentina and Chile had to set aside their arguments about sovereignty, while all had to see the recently vanquished Japan as a reborn nation. The other countries involved were Australia, Belgium, Germany, New Zealand, Norway, and South Africa. The public justification for continuing the research by these 12 countries beyond 1958 was the value and interest of the science, although the real reason was to limit the militarisation of Antarctica by the Soviets and the Americans. There was little interest shown by anyone at government level in the investigation of the more emotional aspects of the continent, but, in fairness to most of those concerned with organising these national activities the humanities were not among their original terms of reference.

It is to the immense credit of the US National Science Foundation (NSF) that it had already seen that its educational remit was an opportunity to involve non-scientists in a different form of exploration of the continent. During IGY, NSF sponsored Leland Curtis, a painter and also a well-known mountaineer, to take part in Operation Deep Freeze. His first visit to Antarctica had been with the US Antarctic Service Expedition led by Admiral Byrd in 1939–1940 and I suspect it was Byrd's influence that meant he was invited back in 1957. The US Navy sponsored the civilian, Robert Charles Haun, and the military artist, Commander Standish Backus. These three produced a wealth of material that not only provided landscapes, but also captured many of the activities of the logistic and science teams.

The UK had no official interest in supporting non-scientists and it was entirely by chance that the Duke of Edinburgh, on a round the world trip aboard the Royal Yacht *Britannia* in 1956, took with him a well-established artist, Edward Seago, to both record his impressions and help teach the Duke to paint. Their visit to the Antarctic Peninsula and South Georgia provided many fine visualisations of ice and grey seas but since the paintings belonged to the Duke, few people ever had the chance to see them until an exhibition at the Scott Polar Research Institute in 2006.

Ad hoc arrangements went on being made which allowed particular individuals to unofficially piggyback the Antarctic logistics operations. It is said that the poet Donald Finkel managed to go south after he met Phil Smith, the Deputy Director of Polar Programs at NSF on a caving expedition, while the Australian artist Sidney Nolan was invited by the US Navy in 1964! NSF recognised that it could incorporate a small number of humanities people within its annual science programme, and by 1969 it had established a more formal relationship for inviting participants. Two early ones were Charles Neider and Louis Halle, both writers whose books on their experiences began to make not only the science but also the experience of living there more publically accessible.

During the 1970s, the US programme slowly picked up speed with Daniel Lang, a landscape painter, followed by the photographer, Eliot Porter, and then a multimedia artist, James Westwater. Most of the support in the 1980s went to writers, who appear to have been commissioned to go south, but by 1989 NSF had instituted a formal competitive system of application with a judging panel which chose to send three of the 18 applicants south.

Seeing the success of the US initiative, other countries recognised that here was an unrealised opportunity. First the Australians decided to start a humanities programme of their own and in 1984 sent an artist, Alasdair McGregor, and a sculptor, Stephen Walker, south. For the first decade or so, they continued to provide two places a year but over the years this has gradually increased so that up to four people have taken part across several summers.

New Zealand had been commissioning artists to visit Scott Base for some years but its official programme had its genesis in the resolution passed by the Antarctic Treaty Consultative Meeting in 1996. This suggested that the support of artists, writers and musicians could help to promote the aesthetic values of Antarctica. They began with two poets, Bill Manhire and Chris Orman, and an artist, Nigel Brown, and since then have taken a very broad view of who could participate, including a fashion designer, a ceramicist, a choreographer and a textile artist, as well as the more generally expected photographers, writers and painters.

Late on the scene came the UK. Having already hosted a number of invited participants, including artist David Smith and composer Peter Maxwell Davies, and observing the major increase in outreach possible through connecting with the artistic public, I persuaded the British Antarctic Survey (BAS) and the Natural Environment Research Council (NERC) to agree to an allocation of two places each summer derived from competitive applications. To help in choosing the participants, BAS entered into an agreement with Arts Council England (ACE) to include the two places in their international fellowship system. We began the scheme in 2001–2002 with two well-established artists (Keith Grant and Philip Hughes) and ran it until 2008–2009 when the ACE abandoned its scheme and support. Sadly, the rapidly shrinking BAS budget and the major cuts to the ACE budget bode ill for any chance of its reinstatement in the immediate future. Meanwhile, various other countries – for example Germany, Argentina and Norway – have seen the advantages of this small investment in diversity and begun to host artistic visits to Antarctica and the results of this have been visible in major exhibitions in Bremen, Buenos Aires and Tønsberg.

Introducing artists and writers into a scientific community is not always easy. One of the problems is that the scientists, who are competing for space on ships and research stations, see this as taking important scientific opportunities away and have commented, not always implicitly, that the outputs from the humanities participants cannot be as important or applicable as those from the science denied. Certainly in BAS, this was an initial reaction from a considerable number of scientists at the inclusion of Maxwell Davies in the 1997–1998 season, and again at the start of the official programme in 2001. This unthinking and positively tribal response was gradually eroded by interaction with the artists and writers and a growing appreciation of how they could use the opportunity as a platform to explain elements of the science to an unscientific audience.

Selecting participants for this BAS programme was never easy. Once we had it fully up and running and advertised, the application rate was normally between 30 and 50 for the two places every season. I chaired the selection panel, but the voting participants were all from the disciplines covered by the applications, and to them we later added one of the previous successful applicants. ACE initially had a problem with the insistence by BAS that all forms of art were eligible for inclusion, a range that embraced what ACE described as 'crafts' and therefore outside what they felt was their remit. Since all members of the panel had to vote on all types of project, the selection of the top two was always a contentious and well-argued decision.

Why should the inclusion of humanities in these government expeditions prove so difficult? C. P. Snow's description of the fields of arts and sciences as the 'Two Cultures', back in 1956, had been meant to help build bridges between what were apparently exclusive mindsets produced by the British educational system then. Change had clearly been slow in coming, as the narrow blinkers of territorial remit were applied by scientists to what should have been seen as a liberating extension of how we use and view the Antarctic. Lynne Andrews has pointed out that "The arts are important to our spiritual survival. Recognition of a place for the arts and humanities in Antarctica could now counteract the upsurge of scientific and technological knowledge that developed at the beginning of the twentieth century, thus forging a closer more balanced relationship between the 'two cultures' of science and art" (Andrews, 2007).

Let me first take issue with those who would see the inclusion of artists as somehow undermining the importance of science. Science as an activity has developed an imperialistic approach to its role in the world, ably assisted in some respects by a remarkably ignorant media whose approach has been largely, "men in white coats speak words of truth even if you do not understand them". Despite the efforts of some talented science writers, the majority of our reporting via newspapers, magazines and television is by journalists with little or no scientific background. While not understanding the details of what they are reporting on, they nevertheless realise that twenty-first century life is based on science exploited through technology, and thus science must play a major role in our present and future happiness. Given the modern insistence of politicians on evidence for decision making, on government funding for science teaching and research, and the general belief among the public that there is a scientific fix for all our ills and mistakes, it is little wonder that scientists innately view themselves as important and as playing a major role in society. The recent changes in arts funding *vis-à-vis* science funding simply underline this. In such a context, one might ask just how can art compete in making a contribution to the general good?

Science provides but one element of our vision, both at home and in Antarctica. To see the world in all its complex and various interactions, we must recognise a wider, deeper and broader role for the human mind and imagination than that constrained by the limits of logical deduction. Without emotional colour, sounds, sights and smells the world as we know it does not really live for us, remain in our memory, and provide an emotional glow of happiness or the sharp pain of injury or unhappiness. Looking at Antarctica exclusively through the lens of science is to see it entirely in two dimensions and only in black and white. It is our other senses that need to be engaged to provide the colours, the resonance, the beauty that makes it memorable and complements the data that we gather. In this, the visions of artists, writers and musicians must play an increasing role as can those of scientists themselves who have artistic talents.

The primary element, powering all of science and arts, is the question of understanding, of knowing something new about an aspect of our world and its inhabitants, of finding a way of describing this new information and constantly looking for new tools to allow different aspects to be investigated and portrayed. In a nutshell, creativity drives both science and art, and although we have managed to systematically drive a wedge between them through our education systems and our simplistic characterisation of their values – science hard and logical, arts soft and emotional – it is a false construction. Yet it persists not least because the two groups find comfort in these rudimentary descriptors. How can artists be logical when their job is to capture emotion and the essence of being? How can we allow scientists not to be logical when they deal only in facts and not in feelings?

Defining creativity has always been a problem as its meaning varies with the cultural context in which it is placed. Artistic creativity has always been considered as a personal and intuitive process, but lacks a generally agreed definition. For present purposes, I would consider it no less organised within rules than scientific creativity, although the rules might well be the constraints of the medium, the technical limitations of the practitioner and the genre within which the output is being created. Generally, what is created is unique and original, capable of describing the interaction between the artist and the subject and of interpretation often in a variety of ways. For some, scientific creativity is merely problem solving, the application of logic to a particular set of facts. But for many others, like Max Planck and Albert Einstein, truly new ideas are not generated by deduction but by imagination, by leaping across existing thinking to find new links and associations. It would be wrong as well to ignore the importance of chance in scientific progress. There are many examples of this as the basis of major discoveries – Newton and the falling apple for gravity, Fleming and the contaminated growth medium for the discovery of penicillin, Fahlberg's discovery of saccharin, and so on. The creative element here is both to see the unexpected and to recognise how it might be exploited.

In essence, perhaps we could describe creativity as the generation of new ideas by critical thinking and emotional initiative, using both data and tools but not necessarily in the way they were originally intended. According to the *Oxford Dictionary*, the word was not coined until 1875 when it was first applied to the imagination of poets. Now we routinely apply it to a wide range of activities including those of management focus groups, the generation of artistic concepts, and the delineation of new scientific paradigms. Most importantly, the act of creativity in any field provides an original solution, a unique interpretation or a new idea.

While the original Renaissance view of the world was holistic, as knowledge developed the world became too complex for it to be the province of a single mind. By the late eighteenth century, a fissure had begun to open between science and arts with the classically educated claiming superiority over the parvenu scientists and technologists. Science became steadily more specialised and the classicists began to claim that while a scientific education could provide a valuable specialist, it could not produce an 'educated man'. By the twentieth century, this distinction between arts and sciences was not only clear in the public mind but had been enshrined in the education system as two cultures.

Yet, as we know, many scientists are visual artists, musicians or writers as well, so they clearly can cope with channelling their innate creativity into other pathways beside the formal rules of science. Many of these have lacked formal training in the artistic disciplines, yet if we look at the Antarctic outputs, for example, in painting we can see considerable natural talent. Perhaps the most striking difference between an amateur and a professional is not simply the rather more gauche way in which the final work is often finished (due perhaps mostly to a lack of practice) but the more general lack of experimentation with the forms used. In this context, the government-sponsored programmes support professional artists, writers and musicians who are experimental and have brought a quite different approach to art in Antarctica than we have evidence of from a century ago.

With no native population, and indeed a transience of occupation throughout the continent, there can be no *in situ* Antarctic cultural development of art as

+ **Flying to Sky Blu.** Philip Hughes, *2002,* Acquacryl and gouache on paper, courtesy of private collection

This approach to landscape, minimalist and forensic, bridges the gap between the first Antarctic artists of the nineteenth century, who interpreted the landscape in a naturalistic tradition, and the neutral satellite photos of the twenty-first century, which provide the objectivity of the instrumental approach.

is evident in almost all countries around the world. Instead, Antarctic art is based on the importation of trends and techniques from many countries then applied to a single area. This approach of bringing together a wide range of nationalities and techniques into a single place has been used very successfully before by artist co-operatives, for instance, the Artists for Nature Foundation (www.artistsfornature.com) has approaches to multiple interpretations of a single place, for example the Copper River Delta in Alaska (Ehrlich et al. 1998). As previously noted, although collaboration between artists and scientists was commonplace in the eighteenth and much of the nineteenth century, the invention of photography largely undermined the need for paintings of landscapes and objects. Yet, while it can be argued that the early paintings from expeditions such as those of Cook or Wilkes were simply the equivalent of documentary records, they were still individual interpretations of the subject in terms of context, colours and proportions in a way that a simple photograph is not. Initially the camera was used as a recording mechanism, but by the time that Ponting and Hurley were using their skills in the Antarctic its creative abilities had begun to be realised. US writer and curator William Fox has asserted that it was the work of the Swiss photographer Emil Schulthess during IGY (Shulthess 1960) that produced a Renaissance movement in terms of photographic interpretations of the Antarctic landscape (Fox 2005).

There are many books of, and about, Antarctic photographs, both modern and historical, which have allowed the development of a degree of critical assessment. This is much more difficult at present, as it is still difficult to find good reproductions of much of the art that has been made and the originals themselves are not only widely spread around the world but also many are in private collections. Thus the literature discussing the history of Antarctic art and its development is fairly sparse. Much of the published material is in the form of ephemeral exhibition catalogues, like Walton & Pearson (2006), on British Antarctic art from 1775 to the present day; those dedicated to a single artist like

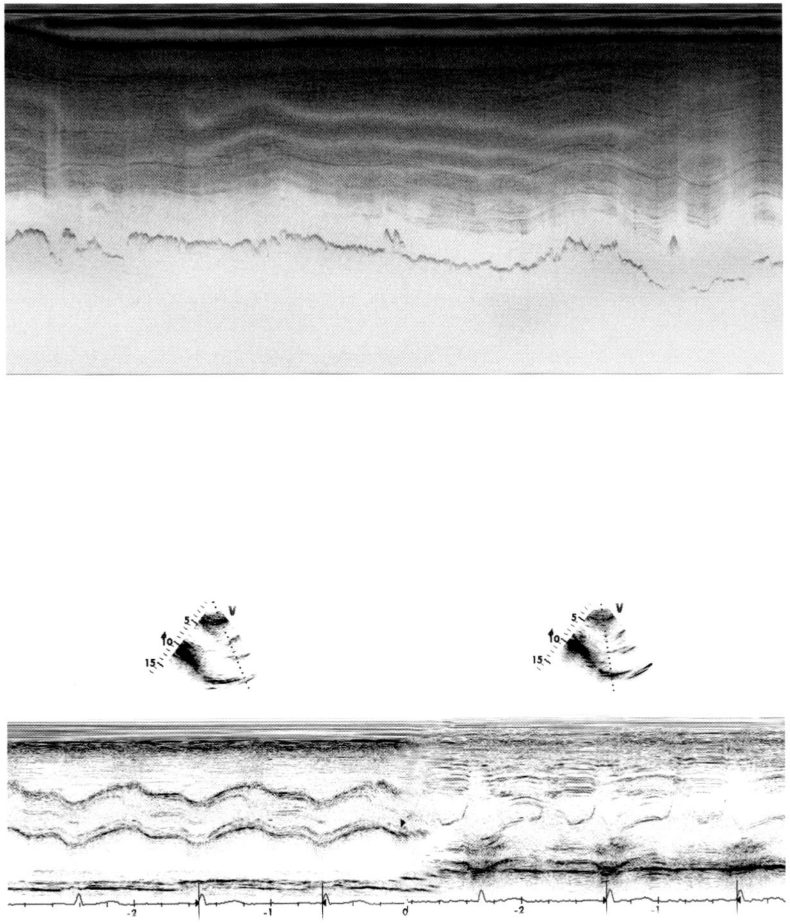

+ **Ice and heart echoes**, Chris Drury, *2007*

Combining science data to produce an artistic original, a new framework for thinking about what we do and know is well illustrated by Chris Drury in his "Double Echo" piece (page 031). Illustrated here are the radio-echo sounding traces that indicate the structure of the rock beneath the ice sheet, as well as the echocardiogram of the pilot flying the aircraft. Separately they are scientific information but when combined alert us to the heart beat of man and the earth superimposed.

Grant (Grant 2003), Hughes (Hughes 2003), Nolan (James 2006), Schmeisser (Hansen 2003), etc; or the recent volume from South America bringing together a variety of Antarctic artists in one volume with both Portuguese and English commentaries (Hug 2009). All of these are of limited distribution and availability. There are a few retrospective volumes, like those by Keith Shackleton (1986), Wally Herbert (2007) or the one on Edward Seago's Antarctic paintings (Dowdswell & Lane 2006), but most of them are documentary rather than analytical or critical. William Fox's book is the most general and analytical approach, although perhaps emphasising the American input rather more than that of other countries. His web chronology is incomplete but a very useful guide to the timeline of participation. Lynne Andrews' volume is the most detailed and the most lavish so far, with an interesting introduction to some of the historical themes, a section on the photographers and artists of the Heroic Age (including Ponting, Wilson, Hurley, Amundsen and Marston) but with the main emphasis on 11 recent artists of whom two are British (David Smith and Edward Seago) and nine are Australian. Recent productions have been a volume compiled by Kathryn Yusoff (2008) where bipolar developments in arts and science were brought together, and an exhibition by Chris Drury (2008) in which he explores the unseen landscape below the ice, using scientific data as the basis for his visualisations.

One collaboration between science and art was the book published by Fogg and Smith, with Fogg writing the text and Smith providing artwork as illustrations. It was through Smith's paintings of fenland winter landscapes that he was invited to visit the Antarctic with BAS in 1975–1976 and again in 1979–1980, while Fogg made several visits as the Chairman of the BAS Scientific Advisory Group. Seeing David Smith's paintings stimulated Fogg to approach Smith to collaborate. Fogg (Fogg & Smith 1990) explains how he feels that the increasing pace of research, the lack of time for scientists to contemplate the scene and think creatively and the stress by managers on not 'wasting time hanging around' has deprived many people of the opportunity to really see the Antarctic and appreciate its non-material qualities. Smith, on the other hand, emphasises how the colours in the Antarctic "would have entranced the great Impressionist painters such as Monet, Renoir, Pissarro and Sisley". (Smith 1981). He goes on to emphasise how it is essential to record the scenes with on-the-spot sketches that "capture the spirit of the moment" in three dimensions much better than any photograph. While the book uses some other pictures besides Smith's, it is his paintings, both in oil and watercolour, that so effectively capture the many facets of ice, glinting like a cut diamond as it refracts the light and produces a kaleidoscope of colours. It is this interaction between the painter and the natural world that captures something missing in the photograph, something ephemeral in the rapidly changing scene but extracted and interpreted by the human mind as a moment frozen in time but with continuing significance.

Even within the limited British programme, we have seen a wide range of approaches to Antarctica ranging from the structural landscapes of Philip Hughes and the icy blue palette of Keith Grant, through the abstract patterns of travel of Layla Curtis and the forensic constructions of John Kelly to the miniature scenes created by Chris Dobrowolski. These, together with artists from other countries, show just what pent-up imagination can provide as alternative visions of this apparently colourless continent.

So what now for our visions of Antarctica in the future? The increasing participation of artists and writers from many different countries is building a multifaceted portfolio of styles, interpretations and materials, capturing many of those previously overlooked elements of the Antarctic experience. A century on from Captain Scott and Edward Wilson, we have not only agreed on the international basis for governing Antarctica but its science is now seen as mainstream and critical for future predictions of the impacts of climate change. At last we are building a holistic interpretation of this frozen world, bringing its beauty and relevance home to the public in a much broader approach than previously and in many different countries simultaneously. The opportunities for new insights, for sparking those creative leaps forward, on both sides of the cultural divide, will increase as we continue to mix scientists and artists together in this strange and unforgiving landscape, allowing their minds and ideas to feed off each other. I can only hope that after such a promising start the UK will restart its programme and not get left behind in this search for new understandings, for better communications and for creative ideas that will help mould our future.

References

Andrews, L. (2007) *Antarctic Eye – the visual journey.* Tasmania: Studio One.

Dowdswell, J. & Lane, H. (2006) *The Antarctic paintings of Edward Seago.* Cambridge: SPRI.

Drury, C. (2008) *Antarctica: a Heartbeat of the Earth.* London: Beaux Arts.

Ehrlich, P.R., Ehrlich, A. H. & Ott, R. (1998) *Artists for Nature in Alaska's Copper River Delta.* Lavenham: Wildlife Art Gallery.

Fogg, G.E. & Smith, D. (1990) *Explorations of Antarctica – the last unspoilt continent.* London: Cassell.

Fox, W. L. (2009) *Antarctic image chronology.* http://www.antarctic-circle.org/fox.htm

Fox, W. L. (2005) *Terra Antarctica: Looking into the Emptiest Continent.* San Antonio, Texas: Trinity University Press.

Grant, K. (2003) *Antarctica*. London: Cadogan Contemporary.

Hansen, D. (ed.) (2003) *Jorg Schmeisser: Breaking the Ice.* Hobart: Tasmanian Museum & Art Gallery.

Herbert, W. (2007) *The Polar World: the paintings of Sir Wally Herbert.* Cambridge: Polarworld.

Hug, A. (compiler) (2009) *Arte da Antártida.* Rio de Janeiro: Instituto Goethe.

Hughes, P. (2003) *Antarctica.* London: Francis Kyle Gallery.

James,R. (2006) *Sidney Nolan: Antarctic journey.* Victoria, Australia: Mornington Peninsula Regional Gallery.

Schulthess, E. (1960) *Antarctica.* New York: Simon & Schuster.

Shackleton, K. (1986) *Wildlife and Wilderness: an artist's world.* London: Clive Holloway Books.

Smith, D. (1981) 'Artistic challenge of Antarctica'. *Geographical Magazine 53*, 884-889.

Snow, C. P. (1959) *The Two Cultures and the Scientific Revolution: the Rede Lecture 1959.* Cambridge: CUP.

Walton, D. W. H & Pearson, B. (2006) *White Horizons*. London: Foreign & Commonwealth Office.

Yusoff, K. (ed.) (2008) *BiPolar*. London: Arts Catalyst.

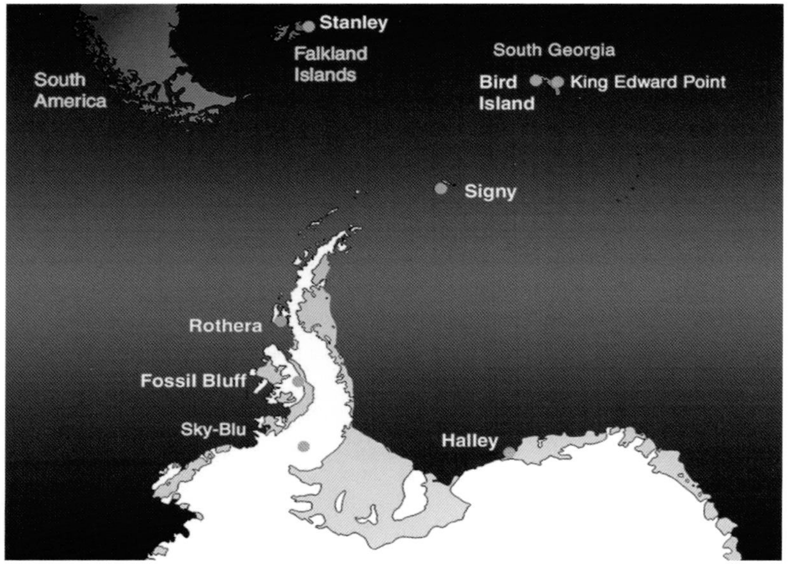

Antarctica is not a scientific curiosity but a key part of Planet Earth. Processes taking place there affect the world's climate and its oceans, and link the continent to all corners of the globe. In understanding climate change, the Antarctic plays a crucial role. The ice sheet preserves a climate and pollution record spanning the last half million years.[1]

. . .

When Francis Drake set out to circumnavigate the world in 1577 little was known about Terra Australia (southern land); it was believed not to exist, to be attached to South America, or to Australia. Drake discovered the passage (now named after him) that proved that no southern continent was connected to Tierra del Fuego, the archipelago forming the southernmost region of South America. Explorers found various islands in the Southern Ocean, the 'sub-Antarctic', during the latter part of the eighteenth and early nineteenth century. This archipelago attracted whalers and seal hunters as well as geographers and cartographers. But nothing was known about the Antarctic itself, so little could be imagined anthropologically, botanically or geographically.

Later expeditions, supported by a number of European nations between them, gradually discovered and charted the Antarctic Peninsula.[2] British ventures (often departing from, or returning to, South America or New Zealand) were active within this and have become legendary. For example, in 1841 James Clark Ross pushed far enough southwards through pack ice to discover the barrier off the Antarctic on the New Zealand side, now named the Ross Ice Shelf. In 1902, the three-man team of Robert Falcon Scott, Ernest Shackleton and Edward Wilson reached 82° 16' 30" South, penetrating further inland than had ever previously been achieved (the *Discovery* expedition). Famously, a few years later in 1911–1912, the Norwegian explorer, Roald Amundsen, reached the South Pole five weeks ahead of Scott who, along with his four-man team, never returned. But, as Ranulph Fiennes is at pains to point out, Scott should be lauded for what he accomplished in terms of scientific discovery, especially in his 1902–1904 expedition, rather than castigated for coming second and failing to make it back (Fiennes, 2003). During this period – often described as 'The Heroic Age' – nations such as Sweden, Germany, Japan and Belgium first made serious attempts at Antarctic exploration. International exploration was a matter of national pride as well as one of individual achievement. The Antarctic is riddled with histories indicated through naming – Ross Ice Shelf, Larson Ice Shelf, Weddell Sea, etc; South Georgia (island) is named after King George III, British monarch at the time of its discovery.[3]

It is hardly necessary to remark on the centrality and significance of geographic exploration and scientific research in the Arctic and the Antarctic. There is also continuing interest in oil and mineral prospects. In 1959, 12 governments, including the British Government, agreed The Antarctic Treaty (in force from June 1961) whereby this region was declared an international zone, an area of scientific

+ British bases in Antarctica. Courtesy, British Antarctic Survey

cooperation and support, used only for non-military purposes.[4] During the latter part of the twentieth century, the speed of development in Antarctic exploration has been immense with many new nations becoming engaged in Antarctic-based research. In the last couple of decades, the peripheral area, particularly the South Shetland Islands and the Antarctic Peninsula, has also emerged as a tourist destination, albeit an expensive one (the Lonely Planet guide to Antarctica was first published in 1996!). The majority of visitors reach the continent by ship, although it is also possible to arrive by plane from Chile or, once in the Antarctic, to fly into the interior. Many of the various national base camps are linked by air.

Nowadays, there is a small science station at the South Pole with several space telescopes, one of which is located some 500m from the pole. The United States Contingent construct a road across the ice, when needed, for ground transportation to move bulk fuel, machinery, and materials to and from this ultimate continental interior. For those of us who have never visited the Antarctic it comes as something of a surprise to see, for example, a photograph of a large grey and metal building, the Amundsen-Scott South Pole Station, rising from the snow, silhouetted against an intensely blue sky (Rubin, 2008: 225).

Research conducted by the British Antarctic Survey (BAS) has been framed rhetorically (since 2009) as 'Polar Science for Planet Earth' and organised under six headings: Polar Oceans, Climate, Icesheets, Chemistry and Past Climate, Ecosystems, Environmental Change and Evolution. Given current debates relating to climate change, one of the goals is "To explain changes in atmospheric circulation, temperatures and sea-ice extent in both polar regions over the past 50 years and to determine how much of this change is due to human activity and how much is a result of natural factors (including solar variability)".[5] The majority of those based in the Antarctic are support workers, facilitating the scientific investigation that remains the primary focus and rationale for investment by various nations including the UK. For artists and writers, opportunities to explore the Antarctic itself remain relatively unusual, and arguably a privilege, one with responsibilities to reflect upon, respond and convey something of the experience of what by all accounts is an extraordinary place.

So what can art do? Writing in 1936, the German Frankfurt School critic, Walter Benjamin, contrasted the healing work of a surgeon with that of a magician, and drew a parallel between this and a comparison of painting and photography (Benjamin, 1936). Where the surgeon cuts into a body (science) the magician performs a sleight of hand (faith/theology); where the photographer penetrates reality (literal representation) the painter critically reflects upon phenomena (conceptual art). Benjamin was writing at the height of the modern era with its emphasis on innovation, experimentation and technological development. His concern was to argue that film (photography and moving imagery) had superseded painting both in terms of its modern (technological) characteristics and, given mass reproduction, its democratic potential to reach wide audiences. We no longer accept such a definitive distinction between art and photography, although, of course, specific media have particular intrinsic properties, potential and limitations. Indeed, it might be argued that various media and modes of expression complement one another in terms of visual means of detailing phenomena and communicating emotional responses to people, places and events.

If this argument is extended, it can equally be suggested that the aims, methods and outcomes of various means of scientific discovery and various media of artistic research may be similarly complementary. Following Benjamin, while surgeons cut into the body, psychoanalysis can tell us something about how such an invasion might feel and artists are concerned with shape, posture and gesture, visual indicators of experiential responses. Likewise, scientists and artists, exploring the same place, may produce complementary results and insights. Aims, methodologies, means of information collection and methods of analysis differ, but they share goals of detailed investigation and discovery. Arguably such differences of objectives, tactics and responses together serve to extend our understanding of the nature of environments such as that of the Antarctic.

The Antarctic is, in many respects, a place of mythology as well as of scientific enquiry. It has figured extensively in the artistic and literary imaginary, often linked to notions of pristine landscapes and the sublime. Particular places inspire geographic imagination through stories told about them. David Hempleman-Adams travelled south in 1995–1996. Introducing *The Heart of the Great Alone,* photography from The Royal Collection associated with Scott, Shackleton and other expeditions, he comments on the psychological challenge both of survival and of achievement of goals in the Antarctic, adding that a key difference between now, and the Heroic Age, is that contemporary explorers know that it is possible to reach the South Pole. (Hempleman-Adams, 2009). He also refers to the 'dramatic stories' of expeditions. Exploration is the stuff of 'Boy's Own' romance, very familiar within English culture of the early to mid-twentieth century. Stories are recounted orally (there is a market in after-dinner talks about exploration). They also escalate rhetorically – Amundsen's account of his 1910–1912 journey prosaically entitled *The South Pole, An Account of the Norwegian Antarctic Expedition in the Fram* (the name of their ship) was re-published in 2007 as *Race to the South Pole*! Amundsen's writing is not in terms of 'race' but in terms of challenge and discovery. Indeed, in so far as there was a sense of competition between nations, surely what explorers have in common more than outweighed any sense of rivalry back home. Amundsen left the Norwegian flag at the South Pole, literally staking a claim, but he also left a note for Scott, fully expecting him to be the next person to arrive there.

Histories are chronicled in journals alongside scientific notes and more mundane everyday experiences or narrated visually through sketches, photography and film. Herbert Ponting's photographs of the *Terra Nova* icebound or Frank Hurley's various photographs of *The Endurance* (1915), yet another tall mast ship marooned within the ice pack, bring a shiver to the spine as we imagine how it might feel to be frozen into the ice for the winter months. Ponting was the first professional photographer to join an Antarctic expedition. Scott's hut at Cape Evans included a darkroom for his use. (Hempleman-Adams, 2009) The resulting photography undoubtedly benefited from the in-depth investigation facilitated by the length of his stay (in effect a precursor of the type of residency recently sponsored by BAS). By contrast with Hurley's silver prints in documentary idiom, Ponting used carbon prints to enhance tonal subtlety, the aesthetic contributing to expressing something of the sublime nature of the environment; he included many landscape studies alongside more detailed photographs of wildlife and of the expedition team. He later experimented in reprinting images on different coloured papers in order to more precisely express the sublime colours he perceived in the Antarctic landscape reflects detailed observation, notes and memories that are unlikely to be accumulated through a short visit (for example,

\+ ***Terra Nova* Icebound,** Herbert Ponting, *13 December 1910,* Courtesy, The Royal Collection © 2011, Her Majesty Queen Elizabeth II

the few days experienced by tourists on Antarctic voyages).[6] That we can imagine the Antarctic as a physical place has as much to do with ways in which it has been pictured as with verbal description or poetry.

Historically, art has mediated geographic and scientific exploration. Ships' crews regularly included artists (later photographers) alongside cartographers whose role was to visually represent that previously not known – at least to the Western world. A huge amount has been published on the subject of polar exploration, including explorers' journals, biographical accounts and historical overviews (often including illustrations by painters, photographers and cartographers); scientific and geographic data; artists' books and exhibitions. Titles are often evocative, for example, *The Heart of the Great Alone* (Hempleman-Adams, 2009) on Scott and Shackleton, or *I May Be Some Time* (Spufford, 1996) on ice and the English imagination. The role and responsibility of artists has changed over time. While we may interpret Edward Wilson's extensive series of Antarctic drawings and paintings from 1902–1904 and 1910–1912 in terms of mood, aesthetics and artistic style, he would have viewed them as primarily informational – as well as recreational, as a personal pastime.[7] Pictures stimulate the geographic imagination, contributing to formulating perceptions of places. More recently, artists have operated as educators, drawing attention to that which might otherwise be ignored. For many scientists this is the primary function of art, or of non-scientific writing. But arguably art, at its best, transcends reportage. As an expressive mode of communication art may operate more or less explicitly – or rhetorically – to shift or enhance understanding of place and circumstances.

A number of the national Antarctic programmes, including the British Antarctic Survey, Cambridge, UK, have commissioned residencies, lasting from a few days to two–three months, whereby artists (visual artists, writers, musicians) have had the opportunity to explore and express something of their experiences and responses to Antarctica and also to live and work alongside scientific teams. The journey is psychological as well as geographical. Attempts to absorb the immensity of the experience, to make sense of the Antarctic as a place start with advance research and planning, and continue after returning home. As Paul Rodhouse, marine biologist and painter, has commented:

> Back in my studio in Cambridge further thought processes go on as I re-run the paintings I have made in my head and then refer to my sketches, notes and digital images. I never start working on a canvas until I have thought through in some detail how I am going to approach a painting. This is not to say that my work always ends as it was first conceived – there are many unexpected turns and happy accidents which I gladly seize upon and exploit in the pursuit of an original finished work.[8]

Different art forms involve differing work methods. Painters or printmakers, such as Philip Hughes, Keith Grant, Chris Drury and, indeed, Paul Rodhouse, rely on sketches, photographs and workbooks, including written notes as memory aides, when developing full scale paintings back in a studio. By contrast photographs and video have to be shot *in situ* (although edited later), which raises questions about the reliability of the range of equipment likely to be needed. This was a key concern, for instance, for the five video camera set-up used by David Wheeler, and for effective sound recording and smooth camera movement when flown on kites in Neville Gabie's project! Nowadays, with digital technology, material can be reviewed on the spot. In the days of film, photographers such as Hurley or Ponting had to maintain a darkroom along with dry and stable temperature storage conditions for undeveloped film, developed film, and prints.[9] By contrast, now the visual record may be instantaneous: Simon Faithfull's palm pilot drawings, or Layla Curtis' journey line, offered immediate webcast expression of their experience of the journey south. Likewise, sculpture and installation based on object collection relies on access to particular places. John Kelly collected stones and botanical samples, Craig Vear sampled sounds of the Antarctic. Installation art, such as Anne Brodie's messages in bottles or Chris Dobrowolski's sledge depend on advance planning, and on chancing possibilities – Brodie took bottles with her and Dobrowolski packed a load of old picture frames, both no doubt puzzling customs officers and those loading the ship. Artists respond to what they find, for example, although Dobrowolski had been collecting Antarctic ephemera in advance of the trip he did not know that packing boxes are still marked 'man food' (although there is no longer a need to distinguish from dog food).

While all artists pursued research in advance, both to try to anticipate what might occur in practical or emotional terms and also to take a relevant range of equipment, there was always an element of serendipity. Art, concerned with place and the nature of specific environments, articulates philosophical reflection, practical strategies, and determination to respond to what is actually *seen* or experienced, in order to avoid making work blinkered by preconceptions. The ability to engage with the unexpected, or with that so sublime that our emotional responses cannot be imagined even if we know in advance that, for instance, luminosity or sheer mountainous scale are characteristic of a particular place, is crucial to an artist's endeavour to communicate that which reaches beyond what might previously have been imagined.

Most of the artists commenced their residency with a flight from the UK to the Falkland Islands, then a journey by sea from Stanley (the exception was Neville Gabie, who, through an accident of timing, travelled from South Africa which is his country of birth so it seemed appropriate). Travel from Stanley was on board either the *James Clark Ross* or the *Ernest Shackleton*. In several cases the journey occupied more than half the time allocated for the residency and most of the artists comment on it, either through making work about the travel experience or through notes in journals and sketchbooks.

Hence the journey formed a part of discussions with me during meetings or studio visits (winter 2010–2011). It was clearly a particular type of social negotiation. Several involved themselves with routine onboard tasks including loading and unloading, and everyone variously socialised with the ship's captain and crew and with the range of scientists and Antarctic base support workers also on board. It seems some longer lasting links developed; David Wheeler remarked that the first officer from *James Clark Ross,* the ship on which he travelled, subsequently made a point of coming to see his exhibition (in Halifax, UK, 2010). One of Anne Brodie's videos shot in the ship's bar effectively indicates evening life on board, as we hear snatches of conversation while watching a gin and tonic heeling with the ship. Similarly, Layla Curtis' close up video of the movement of her soup in the bowl invites us to wonder at the difficulties of moving around, talking or eating on board as the whole ship rolls with the extreme waves.

As a time-based medium, video is ideally suited to indicating something of the experience of constant movement, of the ship itself or of the landscape through which it is passing. David Wheeler's five cameras, set up in a row on deck, not only record the environment through which the ship is moving, but also indicate something of the experience of looking out from on board. Likewise, Neville Gabie's continuous process of sketching shapes through line drawing on a bridge window during daylight not only tells us something about the shape of the ice silhouetted against the horizon, but also reminds us of the claustrophobia that many hours confinement in a cabin can bring. Simon Faithfull's video records one minute a day of the 44 days he spent at sea, as his journey to the Antarctic (where in the end he only spent five nights) was thwarted by inclement weather. We empathise with the cabin fever that we imagine this produced, while knowing that the tasks of daily recording, in video or by palm pilot, will have mitigated this. Several of the artists commented on the necessity of routine professional tasks for everyone, both on board ship and when based in the Antarctic itself. Simon Faithfull made a daily drawing that was embedded in an email sent to over 3,000 people (or institutions) worldwide. He commented on the challenge of making "a record of me being at that point and attempting to filter the world through my head and getting it down as a set of lines". He was using a palm pilot so the sketches tended to be details rather than big, and always minimalistic. He commented on the process as "an absurd proposition to go to Antarctica and attempt to capture it by such limited means". The drawings work minimally to trigger imagination through poetic ellipsis; there is more white space than pixellated lines. Yet, through giving a series number and a location (including latitude/longitude) a running account of the journey was set up, with the images subsequently displayed as postcards, a slide carousel, or on illuminated laser edge plastic.

Likewise, Layla Curtis deployed available technologies, generating a web-based track mapping her journey that was instantaneously and globally accessible. In this respect, self-appointed tasks of journal writing or making work served on the journey and in the Antarctic to introduce professional order into what might otherwise be a set of emotionally chaotic experiences. Routines of investigating, measuring, recording, interpreting and calculating, or running support services such as transportation or canteens, all involving various deadlines along with regular maintenance tasks, operate at one level to steady what might otherwise be overwhelmingly sublime responses to the vast *terra incognita* of the southern waters and continent.

South of the Falkland Islands, there is a Convergence Zone 20–30 miles wide where the warmer waters of the South Atlantic meet the cold waters of the Antarctic, usually producing a region shrouded in mists and fog. Apparently, both the air and sea temperatures drop rapidly as the ship enters the Antarctic Circumpolar Current, the world's greatest ocean current. For first time visitors this must be an unnerving experience, akin perhaps to an eclipse of the sun or similar sublime natural phenomena. Anne Brodie commented that she understands why it is important for organisations to have an outline of what you intend to do when you are there, but that it becomes a hugely personal journey and how the environment affects you as a human affects your work. She remarked, "we're very small and transient; this can make mark-making (for example, drawing) seem pointless as it won't last". John Kelly, for whom the experience opened a 'poetic pulse', commented that it is not only difficult to come to terms with the scale of what confronts you but also to deal with it afterwards, to adjust when you come back. Aside from existential considerations, how the environment actually affects materials may be difficult to anticipate. Brodie often works with that which she finds *in situ*, so tracing paper and plastic became materials – ephemeral and translucent – but the tracing paper curled up in the Antarctic environment. Among the artists, she was perhaps the most focussed on people and place. The glass bottles that she took with her and handed out to those at the base camp were intended to solicit responses relating diverse experiences of working there.

The everyday experience of living and working on board ship, and, more particularly, in the Antarctic, attracted a range of comments from the various artists. The majority spent time at Rothera, the main British station, although John Kelly was at the small summer-only base on Signy Island. Simon Faithfull went via South Georgia to Halley, Neville Gabie also went to Halley and the writer Jon McGregor failed to get to Rothera at all because of ice. Chris Drury became interested in the surface of the ice, remarking that winds have a vortex pattern at Rothera and scour the ice of snow which makes delivery runways possible (no doubt one of the reasons why the base has developed there). It is the largest base and the one most accustomed to visitors, for example, television crews.

Halley, which was established as a physical science station in 1956, is built on a floating and moving iceshelf and is now in its sixth version (as most of the earlier stations have been buried and squashed flat by the annual accumulation of snow). The latest version (completed in 2011) is built on skis, so that the modules can be towed inland each year to keep them from floating out to sea. Buildings at the bases are colour coded according to their precise use, but the skis have to be white as colour absorbs warmth and would dissolve the ice beneath. One of the artists described colour as 'an imposter' in terms of Antarctic phenomena and the response of light rays. For artists as visual thinkers, the visual impact of colour interrupting an otherwise white land palette, begs reflection.

One relatively common difficulty for the artists was their dependence on the generosity of support workers for transport to places that they wished to explore, moving between base camps, or from ship and base. For safety reasons, no one leaves a camp alone and all expeditions have to be notified. Trips out could mean waiting for several days hoping for space on a plane. If weather is adverse, flights are cancelled. Jean McNeil makes use of this as a plot development point in *The Ice Lovers,* when a pilot and a young woman scientist find themselves stranded due to a technical fault, with no possibility of a repairs mechanic being flown in through the fog. The artists often had to wait for a space on a plane, but it seems it was worth the wait; for example, everyone who went to Sky Blu made work in response to the experience and recounted stories of its pristine vistas and scale. This is a distant camp up on the plateau on an area of blue ice about three hours flight from Rothera, used primarily as a refuelling stop for planes flying on to Halley, the Ellsworth Mountains or even the South Pole itself. David Wheeler found himself in this isolated spot at Christmas, at the height of Antarctic summer. Philip Hughes derived several of his larger paintings from his experience of being there and Chris Drury also took the opportunity of a flight to the Ellsworths, one of the most remote mountain ranges in the world.

Opportunities and working relationships were partly a matter of chance. Chris Dobrowolski's decision to bring picture frames with him might be interpreted as questioning how art might be made relevant, how the experience of the Antarctic might be 'framed', as well as providing him with material for transformation. The 12-foot long sledge that he made there was designed and constructed with support from one of the sledge maintenance men familiar with traditional sledge-building; a budget restriction had meant the next sledge-building project was cut, so he had spare time.

Chris Drury shared a room with a field assistant who helped him plan his snow drawings, and he also talked extensively with the scientist responsible for glaciological echo soundings. This became pivotal in his work, as the camaraderie led to access to data that could be extracted for his prints. Drury's interest in things that cannot be seen, but can be visualised by other means, relates to the abstract systems sometimes characterising scientific measurement. That data from instrumental technologies developed for scientific research or for navigation purposes, facilitate graphic rendering of that which cannot be literally detailed testifies to further disciplinary cross-over as the visualisation also informs nature research, for example, expressing the flight path of an albatross. In terms of investigation, Drury's renderings also complement figurative representations of the bird, for instance, Keith Grant's paintings.

Albatrosses are huge birds (stuffed examples in various Antarctic or Natural History museums testify to their sheer size). Conveying a sense of their import within their surroundings, and the sheer geographical range of their territory is challenging. Both Grant and Drury collected information systematically through notes and sketches (for paintings made later) or through technical data extraction. But their choice of subject matter is hardly neutral; the albatross resonates mythically as a sublime creature, an omen of either good or bad luck, and a metaphor for human attitudes to the natural world. In Samuel Taylor Coleridge's poem (1798), the Ancient Mariner's ship is becalmed, cursed as a result of killing the albatross that was beating its wings behind them. The crew subsequently hang the dead albatross round his neck in place of a crucifix. The symbolism is powerful. His conscience cannot be assuaged. The poem signifies something of the psychological and spiritual journey experienced in voyaging south. In other words, scientific data collection methods and varied methods of visual imaging, along with poetic sensibilities, together offer a complex picture of this large seabird that not only indicates something about the bird itself and its behaviour patterns but also articulates its symbolic import.

The research station is a captive space. As one of the artists commented, "...if you want to come to terms with the reality you have to come to terms with the people who work there". It is an artificial community; there is no indigenous human population nor is there a sustenance relationship with the land. Research involves importing everything that might be needed. One artist commented on the amount of plastic brought in, as everything arrived wrapped in plastic air bags (like department store packaging). Whilst no doubt necessary in transport terms, this can seem environmentally intrusive (although all alien materials are removed from the Antarctic for disposal). Day-to-day realities of living and working do not figure prominently for most of us whose imaginary versions of the Antarctic are probably somewhat more romantic in terms of sublime notions of pristine landscapes. In fact, the community there is a microcosm, a little society with everyone including cooks, mountaineers, pilots, plumbers and electricians, doctors, scientists; "...every time you sat down to eat you found yourself with someone whose world is totally different". People live and work there, with some staying, returning regularly, or staying continuously in order to maintain or support the work of researchers through both winter and summer seasons. Anne Brodie's messages in glass bottles reflect the diverse range of people and responsibilities on the base. Paradoxically, in terms of desire for academic inter-disciplinary cooperation, sometimes there was very little contact with scientists as they were often out in the field for long periods. Indeed, the sheer extent of scientific data collection led several of the artists to remark that they wondered who is determining which data is used and who is taking decisions as to where, when and what to explore further.[10]

Perhaps artists and writers are, by their nature, more socially investigative than some. Many base-camp workers spend two and a half years in the Antarctic, so some had the reaction "oh well, yet another artist" and had little interest in art, in what artists do or in how artists and writers work. In addition, apparently most staff are in their twenties; the artists were generally older. Some viewed artists as taking up science space, both berths on the ship and accommodation on base. As in any community, some people engage with art and artists and others do not see any relevance. Apparently, there were sceptics who viewed the residency programme as a BAS corporate public relations gimmick. Social skills and a willingness to 'muck in' obviously help thaw attitudes as in any semi-institutionalised circumstances. But for people accustomed to a high degree of creative autonomy, the mode of being, especially at Rothera with its summer population of up to 120, must seem frustratingly restrictive and clearly the social dimension posed some challenges for the artists working out ways to benefit from the privilege of close contact and intellectual engagement with scientists of varying disciplines while navigating institutional and personal pitfalls.

But they were not entirely isolated. Unlike in earlier historical periods, satellite communication allows for contact with home. For Layla Curtis and Simon Faithfull, new technology facilitated artworks – the web-based account of her journey and his regular Palm Pilot emails – that could not previously have been envisaged. For Neville Gabie, it allowed for a correspondence with his wife, Joan Gabie, also an artist, which led to a series of drawings based on his emails and her interpretation of his accounts of his experience. In his Antarctic journal, Keith Grant comments extensively on his response to the environment, to the people he encountered at the base camp, to work conditions, but also on missing his family and, towards the end of his trip, looking forward to being reunited with them back home. As an artist now based in Norway, who has made extensive studies of light in the Arctic, he is familiar with the elemental conditions of polar areas and with the demands of representing changing formations of ice, sea, sky, weather, light and colour. Given this experience, his several philosophic comments on the immensity and intensity of such effects and affects in the Antarctic and on the challenge of expressing this through painting, seem all the more significant.

Grant's exploration of polar light in many respects fits within a long tradition in painting of investigating the sublime in landscape. Referencing the Platonic distinction between pleasure and pain, Irish Enlightenment philosopher Edmund Burke reflects on the sublime as an effect of or response to phenomena. He suggested that:

> The passions which belong to self-preservation, turn on pain and danger; they are simply painful when their causes immediately affect us; they are delightful when we have an idea of pain and danger, without being actually in such circumstances; this delight I have not called pleasure, because it turns on pain, and because it is different enough from any idea of positive pleasure. Whatever excites this delight, I call sublime. The passions belonging to self-preservation are the strongest of all the passions.
>
> (Burke, 1759, Section XVIII)

Given our instinct for self-preservation, he suggests that death is the one thing worse than pain. However, in an arts context, as spectators we do not confront actual challenges; rather, what is fascinating is enjoyment of vicarious experiences of pain or danger. Art may be deeply enjoyable precisely because, as audience, we are drawn into contemplation of scary or incomprehensible phenomena without directly encountering them. In the case of artists and writers (and anyone else) undertaking research in places such as the Antarctic the experience of the sublime is more immediate. Again, to quote from Burke:

> The passion caused by the great and sublime in nature, when those causes operate most powerfully, is Astonishment; and astonishment is that state of the soul, in which all its motions are suspended, with some degree of horror... Astonishment... is the effect of the sublime in its highest degree; the inferior effects are admiration, reverence and respect.
>
> (Part Two, Section I)

As Philip Hughes commented, however much research is undertaken in advance, nothing prepares one for the actual experience of being in the Antarctic.

During the Enlightenment, when Burke was writing, humankind was romantically posited as existing in harmony with nature yet, as thinking beings, superior within the order of things. There was a perhaps paradoxical interplay between the desire to comprehend, and pleasure in incomprehensibility, in the gap between what could be seen and what could be known. Notions of the sublime in landscape have extended to encompass concern with industrial sublime, legacies of the modern era (sometimes dystopian) and of nineteenth and twentieth-century socio-economic circumstances that remain marked in derelict industrial places, or those now developed for alternative uses. The notion of gap, inducing admiration, astonishment, wonder or fear, figures in more recent discussions of the sublime. We wonder at the technological, both in terms of phenomena seen or experienced but not understood, and in terms of that which despite the fact that it cannot be perceived influences behaviour patterns. For example, wi-fi invisibly penetrates our everyday space and we can channel surf the television from the armchair. It is indeed the stuff of science fiction – as was once the idea of reaching the South Pole, let alone building a space observatory there!

While many aspects of the Antarctic remain to be explored, it is precisely technological developments that have enhanced ways of charting this vast area. The sounds of the Antarctic, captured by Craig Vear, rely on highly sophisticated recording technologies that complement the classical references of Melanie Challenger's poems or resonate with Jean McNeil's description of the polar landscape as the setting within which the futuristic plot of *The Ice Lovers* is played out. Similarly, David Wheeler's panoramic photograph digitally printed on navigation chart paper, in combination with Philip Hughes' painterly depiction of the sheer immensity of the Sky Blu plateau, enhances our sense of the immensity of space here – we imagine how fearsomely the winds might screech round tents in the temporary camp and the sheer cold of being there. Anne Brodie and Chris Drury recall travelling together to Sky Blu, where their first response was to set about building an igloo; this perhaps says something of the (childlike) pleasures of direct tactile engagement with nature, picking up stones, damming streams, or, in this instance, hewing out chunks of ice to create a hideaway. Brodie subsequently used ice fragments from the igloo to build a structure that was eroded by the wind in only three days. She also brought two ice pieces back from Sky Blu. Scientists bring ice back for analysis, but her doing so resonates more symbolically as they were intended as mementoes. It also testifies to her determination, as bringing ice out involved getting permission, finding a spare box for conveyance, arranging for a 90kg block of ice to travel in an unheated plane from Sky Blu to Rothera, then by ship back to BAS, Cambridge where it is archived for 'non-scientific purposes'.

In trying to grasp something of the sublime immensity and remoteness of the Antarctic, I asked the artists about light, colour and sound. Philip Hughes commented that in summer, it is light all the time, and that this affects you (you never stop working as you can work at four in the morning). Apparently, everything is flattened as the light gradually changes over the course of the day and the colour of the ice is amazing, although he anticipated this. For Chris Drury, as is evident in his prints, the Antarctic is blue; for Layla Curtis it is "as many shades of blue as you can imagine, from greys to turquoise". For Drury it is marked by "persistent, roaring wind; plus, near the sea, the sound of water melt from glaciers". This is particularly manifest in Craig Vear's sound recordings, but is also evident in Neville Gabie's camera kite-flight video when the wind arrests the microphone. Gabie commented on the wind and on the "really cold light", adding that at sunset the place fills with warm tones and hues. For others, the Antarctic is very black and white. Simon Faithfull referred to an "extreme hallucinatory white" commenting that rather than being expansive, there is no horizon so there is a collapsing of space, "it feels like the world has been deleted" rather "like being in a black room with your eyes open". David Wheeler remarked that colour stands out and anything that is large with a bright colour, like a ship, or a human being, helps give scale to where you are.

For all the artists, there was some sense of perceptual disorientation that was simultaneously fascinating and profoundly disturbing. Although David Wheeler also commented that there are "not many times that you are away from sounds of the ship's engines ticking over, or an aircraft, or a generator". In such an expansive space, such alien – yet necessary – noise must blend astonishment with both technological sublime and the environmental. At least engine noise is familiar, even if apparently out of place. Other experiences must be even more unnerving, for instance, apparently it is utterly silent walking along the hills at Fossil Bluff on George VI Sound, as there is no life there, no signs of insect life, no dust, no cobwebs, and only an occasional bird in the air.

Wildlife generally gathers nearer the sea, concentrated in certain areas. John Kelly, who, as is clear from the tonal qualities of his work, is among those who saw the Antarctic as black and white, remarked that at Signy, a remote British research station on a small island in the South Orkney islands, there is quite a lot of exposed rock. Also, much more wildlife than he anticipated: birds as well as penguins (about 25,000) and seals (elephant seals and fur seals). He noted that Antarctic terns, Wilson's storm petrels, skuas, sheathbills and snow petrels were all around. Kelly was based at Signy alongside two penguin researchers, two botanists, a base commander and a maintenance man. He was there for a long period of time and comments that after a few weeks down there they became interested in what he was doing. His background in geology and geography may have helped him relate to the broader context of Antarctic science, although, as he remarked, scientists tend to identify very deep veins of research that are narrow, and tend not to be inter-disciplinary, which is a great limitation when thinking about inter-relations of art and science. Science and contemporary art share the same fundamental goal, that of investigation and discovery. But disciplinary approaches differ markedly, with the sciences generally emphasising specialism and established methodologies, and artists often more open to differing modes of enquiry. Yet there is an emphasis on research through practice in applied science, as there is in contemporary art, that should at minimum offer a parallel emphasis upon discovery and critical reflection, on theoretically informed practice.

In the instance of Antarctica as a last, vast sublime wilderness, perhaps Benjamin's surgeon, artist, and film maker remain metaphorically instructive. Each brings different objectives, modes of creative thinking, and methods into play, together offering a fuller picture of what has occurred. One of the values of artists living in remote places, alongside scientists of various disciplines and expertise, as well as with support teams, is that art can represent place, mediate scientific responses to phenomena and also, crucially, offer different perceptions through which new ways of thinking about and exploring our environment may be generated. Clearly, if this is to be achieved, then investigations have to penetrate beyond the superficial. Hence, the value of longer-term residencies which offer opportunities to study the environment in different weather conditions and through seasonal change, and also to take into account the seasonal rhythms of scientific endeavour. It's with Herbert Ponting's extensive portfolio of Antarctic photography, made over many months, that the work of the British Antarctic Survey artists gained substance and therefore accumulated authority through our sense, as audience, of the seriousness of their research and commitment to communicating impressions, findings and responses through creative practice. All the artists and writers variously comment that the experience continues to influence their work. But the significance of the residency programme goes beyond this as, conversely, their work offers insights that are subjective as well as informational, offering points of identification for us and thereby contributing to general understanding of the nature of the Antarctic as a region and of why Antarctica matters.

Reference

Roald Amundsen (1912) *The South Pole, An Account of the Norwegian Antarctic Expedition in the Fram, 1910–1912*. London: John Murray. Trans. A.G. Chater. Republished (2007) as *Race to the South Pole*. Vercelli, Italy: White Star Publishers

Lynne Andrews (2007) *Antarctic Eye*. Mount Rumney, Tasmania: Studio One

Walter Benjamin (1936) 'The Work of Art in an Age of Mechanical Reproduction' in Hannah Arendt ed. (1970) *Illuminations*. London: Jonathan Cape Ltd

Anthony Brandt ed. (2004) *The South Pole: A Historical Reader*. Washington DC: National Geographic Society

Edmund Burke, from 'A philosophical enquiry into the origin of our ideas of the sublime and beautiful' (1759), in Andrew Ashfield and Peter de Bolla (eds) (1996) *The Sublime, a reader in British eighteenth-century aesthetic theory*. Cambridge CUP

Ranulph Fiennes (2003) *Captain Scott*. London: Hodder and Stoughton

David Hempleman-Adams (2009) *The Heart of the Great Alone: Scott, Shackleton and Antarctic Photography*. London: Royal Collection Publications

Jeff Rubin (2008) *Antarctica*. London: Lonely Planet Publications Pty Ltd. 4th Ed.

Philip Shaw (2006) *The Sublime*. Abingdon, Oxon: Routledge

David W. H. Walton and Bruce Pearson (2006) *White Horizons, British Art from Antarctica, 1775–2006*. London: Foreign & Commonwealth Office

Endnotes

1 John Kelly, Antarctic artist 2003, exhibition invitation, 2006.

2 Given that this is a publication including work by British-based artists supported by the British Antarctic Survey, this extraordinarily abbreviated summary highlights British expeditions. This is not to dismiss the importance of ventures by many explorers from elsewhere.

3 Histories and perceptions may differ, or be contested. Certainly the Falkland Islands/Islas Malvinas are a matter of continuing dispute. It could be argued that this is primarily because, for example, if an oil field is discovered in the Falklands region, British ownership facilitates economic benefits.

4 The others were Argentina, Australia, Belgium, Chile, France, Japan, New Zealand, Norway, South Africa, USSR, USA. There are now 28 nations active in the region.

5 http://www.antarctica.ac.uk/about_bas/publications/pspe.pdf

6 A key example is 'Cirrus Cloud over the Bourne Glacier' 19th December 1911, which he carbon printed onto paper dyed orange, and onto blue, in an attempt to capture actual colours. The orange print is included in *The Heart of the Great Alone*, The Queen's Gallery, London, 2011–2012.

7 The Scott Polar Research Institute archives hold an extensive collection of his work and that of many other polar artists and photographers.
www.spri.cam.ac.uk/museum/catalogue/edwardwilson

8 Paul Rodhouse. http://website.lineone.net/~polar.publishing/paulrodhouse.htm accessed 13.9.11. Professor Rodhouse, marine biologist and painter, is currently responsible for the British artist residency programme, originally set up by Professor David Walton.

9 Ship-borne photography dates from its earliest days; it is known that Sir John Franklin had daguerreotype equipment on board for his fated North West Passage expedition of 1845 (Gordon, in Hempleman-Adams, 2009: 39). The daguerreotypes that Franklin made did not survive so we have no visual record of that trip.

10 On further enquiry, I was assured that this is driven by project proposals subject to international academic peer review, or by long-term data collection (for example magnetic or seismic data) that contributes to a global data system.

Anne Brodie www.annebrodie.co.uk

With a degree in Biology, Anne completed an MA at the Royal College of Art in 2003. Working experimentally with hot glass, film and photography, she jointly won the international Bombay Sapphire prize for design and innovation with a short film, *Roker Breakfast* in 2005. A pivotal shift in her working practice occurred after 2006 when Anne was awarded the British Antarctic Survey/Arts Council Artists and Writers fellowship to Antarctica where she lived and worked at isolated scientific bases for nearly three months. Often working at the boundaries between science and art, her current work explores questions of ownership and the decision making processes involved in what constitutes 'valid data', usually the preserve of scientists. In 2009, Anne was awarded a Wellcome Trust arts award for a collaborative project exploring bacterial bioluminescence and its external relationship with the human body. Her work has been shown nationally and internationally, at venues which include, in London, the Victoria and Albert Museum, The Royal Institution of Great Britain, The Old Operating Theatre Museum, and the Maison Européenne de la Photographie, in Paris.

Layla Curtis www.laylacurtis.com

Layla Curtis is an artist. Her work encompasses a variety of media and often employs technologies such as thermal imaging cameras, Global Positioning Systems (GPS) and video to create drawings and trace journeys. She has exhibited widely, with solo exhibitions at Milton Keynes Gallery (2000), New Art Gallery Walsall (2006) and Ormeau Baths Gallery, Belfast (2008) and group exhibitions at Tate Modern, London; Pavilhão Lucas Nogueira Garcez-Oca, São Paulo, Brazil and CCA, Montréal, Canada. Her work is in the Tate Collection and she has undertaken residencies at AIAV, Japan (1999), Ramsgate Maritime Museum/Turner Contemporary (2004) and Art on the Underground (2007/8). In 2010 she visited the Borneo rainforest to develop new work while walking and living with the indigenous semi-nomadic Penan. Recent projects include a new commission with Film & Video Umbrella.

Chris Dobrowolski www.cdobo.com

Chris Dobrowolski was an artist in residence with the British Antarctic Survey in the 2008–2009 season. Primarily a fine art maker, Dobrowolski has built, flown and crashed his own aeroplane. He has exhibited nationally and internationally but is not represented by a gallery and his work is more often disseminated through performance lectures. In 2006 and 2011 he performed at the Edinburgh Fringe Theatre Festival. He has been a visiting lecturer at a varied and diverse collection of places that include The Ruskin, Oxford University, Musashino Art University Japan and The Royal College of Art, but also village halls and an economics university in Bucharest. He was once deceived into working for the Morale Welfare and Recreation Program (the US military's welfare department).

Chris Drury www.chrisdrury.co.uk

Chris Drury's work makes connections between different phenomena in the world, specifically between Nature and Culture, Inner and Outer and Microcosm and Macrocosm. To this end, he collaborates with scientists and technicians from a broad spectrum of disciplines and uses whatever visual means, technologies and materials are best suited to the situation. He has exhibited worldwide for over 35 years and his work is featured in many key surveys of Land Art. Recent projects include a British Antarctic Survey residency in Antarctica, an exhibition about place, ecology and politics at The Nevada Museum of Art called *Mushrooms|Clouds* and a residency in The Cradle of Humankind in South Africa. Over the last decade, Drury has been working with clinicians to make links between systems in the body and systems on the planet.

Simon Faithfull www.simonfaithfull.org

Simon Faithfull is an internationally exhibited artist whose conceptual practice often incorporates travel. In 2004–2005, he spent two months on board the *RSS Earnest Shackleton* travelling to Halley Research Station, Antarctica. During this journey south, he sent one drawing a day to over 3,000 people around the world via email, as well as producing various video works, photographs and diary extracts. These later became the book *Ice Blink* (published by Bookworks) as well the exhibition and lecture of the same name. Faithfull is a lecturer at the Slade (UCL) and lives and works in Berlin and London. Recent projects include the public artwork *Liverpool to Liverpool* (Liverpool, UK) and a major solo exhibition in Göttingen Kunstverein, (Germany) in 2012.

Neville Gabie www.nevillegabie.com

Neville Gabie spent the summer season 2008–2009 at Halley Research Station on the Brunt Ice Shelf, Antarctica, the first artist to do so. Previous projects include: *Posts,* published by Penguin Books 1999–2006. Up in the Air, artist/curator, Liverpool 2000–2005. Coast-Firstsite Gallery/Commissions East 2003–2005. Right to Play/Art Review commission, Pakistan 2006. Royal Botanical Garden, Hamilton Canada 2008. Cabot Circus, Bristol 2006–2009 Tatton Park Biennial, Manchester 2010. Collections include; Arts Council, Tate Gallery. Artist in residence – MOMART, Tate Liverpool 1999–2000 Vitamin Creative Space, Guangzhou, China – 2004 IASKA, Western Australia – 2005–2006. He is artist in residence for the Olympic Delivery Authority on the Olympic Park, London 2010–2011.

Keith Grant www.chrisbeetles.com

Born in Liverpool, August 1930, Keith Grant worked at the local Co-op and served in the RAF before moving to London, where he studied at Willesden School of Art and the Royal College of Art, gaining a silver medal for mural painting. Since 1960, he has held regular solo shows in London and elsewhere, and for many years taught at leading art schools. Drawn increasingly to northern terrains, he first visited Norway in 1957, and immediately began to incorporate motifs inspired by the country into his work. Returning frequently, he finally settled there in 1996. While seizing opportunities to explore contrasting climes, he remains devoted to the cold north. He is now represented by Chris Beetles Ltd, St James's, London.

Philip Hughes www.philiphughesart.com

Philip Hughes is a painter with a special interest in archaeology, topography and maps. His representation of the land can be seen in two main themes: walking through the land, tracks, marks on tracks; and seen from above, showing the structure of the land and patterns of man's intervention. He has made substantial series of works in the extreme and remote areas of Antarctica, Central Australia and northern Scotland. He has had more than 40 one-man exhibitions, including many in public galleries, in the UK, France, Italy, Mexico and Australia; and his work is held internationally in numerous public galleries and private collections. He spent seven weeks with BAS in 2001–2002, largely based in Rothera.

John Kelly www.johnkellydeepfield.co.uk

Recent work, which includes Flood Cycle and the Inferno project as well as Due South, has focussed upon the interpretation of landscape; recent exhibitions in both museums and art galleries have shown the progression of this through the act of travelling. As a self-taught artist, the work reflects a background in geography and geology. Through fellowships and international residences in the Antarctic and Arctic regions, this work indicates the collaboration that occurs between art and science when in the field, for example, projects benefitting from inputs on glaciation, oceanography and climate change. The result is a new and ongoing relationship with the landscape, through keeping journals and visual diaries, as well as 'forensic' work within the realms of extreme wilderness.

David Wheeler www.ioutheatre.org

David Wheeler is an Artist and is Artistic Director of IOU. With a producing team, he brings together artists, musicians, composers and makers, to make visual, performance and music-based work. David travelled with BAS during three months of the Antarctic summer of 2007–2008, on a journey from Port Stanley in the Falklands to Sky Blu at the southern end of the Antarctic Peninsula. A series of projects has evolved from his experience that focuses on the theme of hidden forces and natural phenomena. These projects include a photographic and video exhibition, a sculpture installation, and performance, sound and music projects. In 2008, David was awarded an Honorary Doctorate from the University of Huddersfield for his contribution to contemporary theatre practice.

Craig Vear www.ev2.co.uk/vear

In 2011, Vear was nominated for an Olivier award and a Canadian DORA award for best sound design for *The Railway Children*. In 2010, he was commissioned by the Laurence Sterne Trust, York Theatre Royal and Arts Council England to compose a digital opera based on *A Sentimental Journey* (1768). In the same year, he was commissioned by Exhibition Road Cultural Group and PRS Foundation to create Flow to celebrate World Music Day and the 25th anniversary of the opening of the Ismaili Centre, London. Superfield [Mumbai] (2009) commissioned by Bradford Mela and Mumbai Festival incorporated found sounds and music from the streets of Mumbai, weeks after the terrorist attacks of 2008. During 2003–2004, he held the Arts Council England Fellowship with the British Antarctic Survey, which resulted in a large-scale composition created from field recordings. In 2006, Unicorn Theatre, London commissioned *Play: Antarctica* about these experiences. In 1997, he co-founded the pop group Cousteau, which made 300,000 sales worldwide and gained a gold disc. Singing Ringing Buoy, an installation at the National Maritime Museum Cornwall (2007–2008), was shortlisted for the 2005 PRS New Music Award.

Melanie Challenger www.grantabooks.com

Melanie Challenger worked in the Falkland Islands, South Georgia, Antarctica, and spent two months on board *RRS James Clark Ross*. Her book, *On Extinction* (Granta: Oct. 2011) narrates her travels to the abandoned whaling stations of South Georgia, the melting icescape of Antarctica, and the Inuit camps of the Arctic, where she traces the links between human activities and environmental collapse. In 2009, she won a British Council Darwin Now Award, and her first collection of poems, *Galatea* (Salt Publishing: 2006), received the Society of Authors' Eric Gregory Award.

Jon McGregor www.jonmcgregor.com

Jon McGregor is a novelist and writer of short stories. He spent six weeks on a research ship travelling between the Falkland Islands, South Georgia, and the Antarctic Peninsula (en route to Rothera, the British research base, which he never reached). His most recent novel is *Even The Dogs* (Bloomsbury). He is an Honorary Lecturer in the School of English Studies at the University of Nottingham, and is still working on an Antarctic novel.

Jean McNeil www.mckernanagency.co.uk

Jean McNeil is originally from Nova Scotia, Canada. She is the author of 10 books, including *The Ice Lovers* (2009), which is set in the Antarctic. She spent three and a half months in the Antarctic with BAS in 2005–2006; she has since undertaken residencies in the Falkland Islands, Svalbard and off the coast of Greenland, on a Natural Environment Research Council-funded ship-based scientific expedition. In 2010, she was a Mellon Foundation scholar at the University of Cape Town, South Africa. She teaches on the MA in Creative Writing at the University of East Anglia. Her latest publication *Night Orders* (2011) collects diary entries, poems and images from the Arctic and Antarctic.

David W. H. Walton www.bas.ac.uk

I joined British Antarctic Survey (BAS) as an ecologist in 1967. For the next 39 years I worked for BAS in a variety of research and management posts, gaining a PhD from Birmingham University, establishing two new science divisions and repeatedly visiting the Antarctic and the Arctic. By 2006, I was responsible for all the environmental management and conservation, mapping, databases and information management, as well as running the Artists & Writers Programme. I was awarded the Polar Medal for my contributions to Antarctic research and the first SCAR Medal for International Scientific Collaboration in 2006. I am a Visiting Professor at Liverpool University, Editor in Chief of the international journal *Antarctic Science*, a trustee of two charities and Chief Rapporteur for the annual meetings of the Antarctic Treaty.

Liz Wells www.landwater-research.co.uk

Liz Wells (curator) writes and lectures on photographic practices. Her book, *Land Matters: Landscape Photography, Culture and Identity* (I.B. Tauris, 2011) offers a contemporary critique of photography relating to land and environment. Exhibitions as curator include *Facing East, Contemporary Landscape Photography from Baltic Areas* (UK tour 2004–2007), Chrystel Lebas and SofijaSilvia in *Conversations on Nature* (Rijeka, Croatia, 2011), *Sense of Place* (BOZAR, Brussels, June 2012) and *Futureland Now* (Laing Gallery, Newcastle, 2012). She is editor of *The Photography Reader* (Routledge, 2003) and of *Photography: A Critical Introduction* (Routledge, 2009, 4th Ed.), and is also co-editor of *Photographies* (Routledge Journals). She is Professor in Photographic Culture, Faculty of Arts, Plymouth University, UK and convenes the research group for Land/Water and the Visual Arts.

Peninsula Arts

Peninsula Arts serves as the arts and culture public programming organisation for Plymouth University, operating from within the Faculty of Arts. The year-round programme includes exhibitions, music, film, public lectures, and theatre and dance/performance.

One of its principal aims is to provide access to a programme of wide-ranging, high quality arts and cultural experiences, informed by the expertise, research and scholarship of Plymouth University and its partners, to the communities of Plymouth and the South West and visitors to the region.

The Peninsula Arts Gallery is a large contemporary arts venue, which aims to showcase a wide range of art and design of distinct national and international interest.

For more information, please visit:
www.peninsula-arts.co.uk

Acknowledgements

Liz Wells would particularly like to thank Professor David Walton and the British Antarctic Survey as well as all the artists and writers whose work appears in this publication. Philip Hughes would like to thank Lord & Lady Gavron, Simona Hughes and Francis Kyle Gallery.

Publisher's Note

Following requests from contributors, some diary entries appear in their original (un-edited) form.

British Antarctic Survey

The Cambridge-based British Antarctic Survey (BAS) is a world leader in research into global environmental issues. With an annual budget of around £45 million, five Antarctic Research Stations, two Royal Research Ships and five aircraft, BAS undertakes an interdisciplinary research programme and plays an active and influential role in Antarctic affairs. BAS has joint research projects with over 40 UK universities and has more than 120 national and international collaborations. It is a component of the Natural Environment Research Council. Between 2001–2009, with funding from Arts Council England, BAS ran an award-winning programme of Antarctic residencies for British artists and writers.

For more information, please visit:
www.antarctica.ac.uk

PENINSULA ARTS WITH PLYMOUTH UNIVERSITY

British Antarctic Survey
NATURAL ENVIRONMENT RESEARCH COUNCIL

MADR